Kate Hastrop

KATE HASTROP has been involved in almost every aspect of home economics including lecturing and examining for several degree and diploma courses. She has worked for many of the major Food Marketing Boards, and for a number of kitchen appliance firms in the UK. Her keen interest in nutrition has led her to research work for Queen Elizabeth College, the Department of Health and the Health Education Council, investigating the problems of nutrition for the elderly and the links between food and health.

Mrs Hastrop has written many books, including two on freezer cookery, and she is a regular contributor and consultant for the BBC in the South of England. Her hobbies are collecting and restoring antiques and renovating old cottages. She lives in Hampshire in a sixteenth-century cottage.

Know Your Onions

Kate Hastrop

Illustrations by Joyce Tuhill

Hamlyn Paperbacks

For Dennis - my husband

KNOW YOUR ONIONS

ISBN 0 600 36765 7

First published in Great Britain 1980
by Hamlyn Paperbacks

Hamlyn Paperbacks are published by
The Hamlyn Publishing Group Ltd,
Astronaut House,
Feltham,
Middlesex, England

Set, printed and bound in Great Britain by
Cox & Wyman Ltd, Reading

Contents

Acknowledgements 6
Preface 7
Introduction 8
History and Folklore 9
Remedies 13
Modern Nutrition 15
How to Grow Your Own 16
How to Store 21
Preparation and Basic Cooking 25
Appetizers and Starters 35
Soups 46
Main Courses 61
Onion Accompaniments 109
Salads 127
Snacks and Savouries 137
Baking 155
Sauces, Dressings and Stuffings 173
Preserves and Pickles 186
Index 199

Acknowledgements

I am indebted to all those who have 'talked onions' with me over the last few months, giving me a wealth of additional information which only added to my enthusiasm, and in particular to those friends whom I talked into compensating for my own shortcomings by helping with drawings, charts and proof-checking. In particular I wish to thank the home economists from the Flour Advisory Bureau, Tower Housewares Ltd and the Metal Box Co. for their immediate response to requests for specialist help, to Jill Nice for the preserve section and to the agricultural specialist who checked my gardening section.

Last, but by no means least, I am grateful for the help and willingness shown by Jean Gale who both deciphered my handwriting in typing the manuscript, and checked the metric/imperial translations in the recipes.

K. H.

Preface

Everyone who enjoys eating well-flavoured food will probably be well aware of the contribution the onion in one form or another has made to the dish.

Everyone who enjoys cooking will, when they think about it, realize our complete dependence on this superb vegetable and members of the onion family.

Everyone who enjoys gardening will probably get one of their greatest 'job satisfactions' from home-growing onions, leeks, garlic, chives, etc.

A couple of years ago the above rather emphatic statements were the beginnings of a conversation my husband and I had together, and almost in unison we said, 'It would make a good book – know your onions.' We laughed!

Whenever we could find a minute my husband gathered relevant, interesting information about the whole onion family and I started collating my favourite recipes, a definite dependence on the 'onion' being the criterion for selection.

My husband died suddenly in the spring of 1978 – the garden and my life will never be quite the same again. This book is dedicated to his memory.

K. H.

Introduction

Of course, if you are as converted to the value of the onion as I am, you will quickly say that there are few savoury recipes that couldn't be included in this book and you would be quite right.

I have therefore, from my massive personal file of recipes, selected those using as a 'minimum' requirement in the ingredients at least *one onion* or other member of the onion family, knowing that without that one onion the recipe would not be the good one it is.

I do not honestly believe there is such a thing as an original recipe, for when I feel I have created an absolutely new combination of ingredients, I find a friend, testing it, will say, 'Oh, I do one like this with pork instead of lamb, rosemary instead of basil, courgettes instead of tomatoes, pasta instead of rice and I pan-fry instead of casserole it – but otherwise it's just the same!' What I am really saying is that all of us interested in the preparation and cooking of food are always modifying existing recipes, either to the time and money available or just to the ingredients to hand, hence often something new and good is achieved almost by accident.

What I would like to do is personally to thank all those professional home economists, cookery writers and enthusiastic personal friends for the inspiration throughout the last twenty years, in persuading me to line the walls of my house with very nearly every cookery book published!

I hope other compulsive buyers of cookery books will include this little book amongst their collection and enjoy using it as much as I have enjoyed writing it.

If I could persuade some of our young generation to buy and experiment with the dishes and *note the flavour*, I would feel I had done my bit in challenging the statistics that say we all like 'bland food' today.

Kate Hastrop

History and Folklore

It is probable that the onion and its near relations are the oldest known vegetables in the world, going back thousands of years.

Onions

The Jews appreciated the onion's virtues when, sighing for the fleshpots of Egypt, they remarked to this effect in Numbers 11: 5, mentioning cucumbers, melons, leeks, onions, and garlic. Some considered the onion divine, even too divine to eat, though Egyptian workmen were said to have eaten them whilst building the Pyramids.

Onions are considered to have Central Asian origins. They were known to the Greeks and Romans. They belong to the lily family and there are two schools of thought about the derivation of the name. One is from the Latin *unio* meaning oneness or singularity, the other is a corruption of *usnio* meaning burning or stinging.

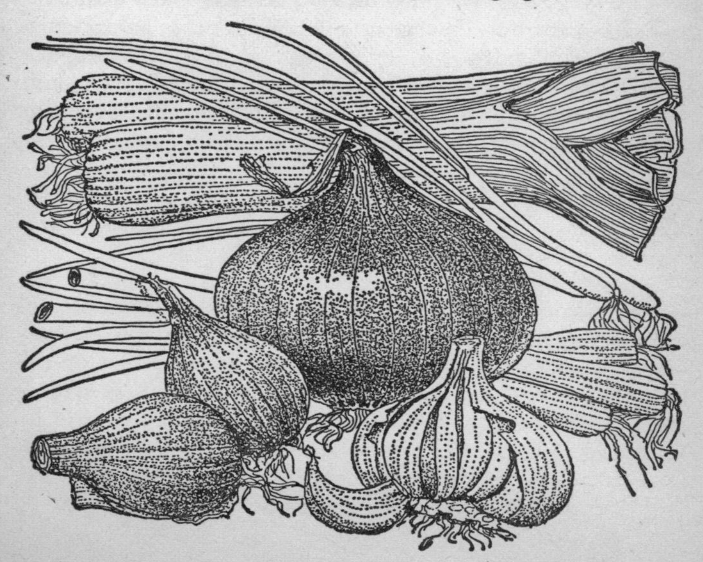

Thousands of years ago, onions were given as a wedding present in the belief that they had aphrodisiac powers, indeed the Greeks again (who seemingly could do nothing without the help of the onion) considered them the most effective erotic stimulant and their comic writer Diphilus stated that as they 'whetted desire they weakened the eyesight', which in some instances was no bad thing presumably!

Superstition has it that one will have a vision of one's future wife if an onion is placed under one's pillow on St Thomas's Eve – December 21st. In South America onions were burnt on the fire for good luck and carried, strapped to one's left arm, to ward off disease.

Countrymen are said to believe that a thick-skinned onion crop indicates a severe winter to follow.

Their origins are not known, but onions must have been held in high esteem for the following phrases still to exist:

1. Spruce as an onion
2. Know your onions – where else would I have found the title for this book?

There is very early mention of bread, cheese and onions being eaten in England and this combination still remains the popular Ploughman's Lunch of today.

In France the famous Onion Soup originated as warming nourishment to early-morning traders at Les Halles, the original equivalent to our Covent Garden wholesale vegetable and fruit market.

Leeks

The origins of leeks are not certain, but it is thought they were cultivated in Egypt in the time of the Pharaohs. They were certainly brought to England by the early Romans. The leek has been the Welsh national emblem since A.D. 640 and is worn by Welshmen even today on St David's Day. It originated when Welsh soldiers, under King Cadwallader, were ordered to wear them in order to distinguish themselves from their Saxon invaders.

If your birthday falls on February 9th, the leek is considered to be your birthday plant!

Old sayings that have been handed down over the years include: 'green as a leek,' and 'not worth a leek,' and to 'eat leek' metaphorically meant to eat humble pie.

Old Cornish recipes refer to the leek as the 'ollick,' though Mrs Beaton declared the leek to be little used in England in 1900 though held in high esteem in Wales.

Competitive growing of leeks for length and girth rather than flavour has been the sport particularly of those living in North East England for many years, with experts weighing leeks in at 4½ kg and more than 50 cm around their blanched base. As judging day gets near their growers are known to put a tent around the plant and 'sleep with it' to combat sabotage.

Even today very serious betting takes place and it certainly surprised me a year or two ago to discover one Newcastle family I met giving credit for all their household luxuries – TV, washing machine, freezer, etc. – to the not so humble leek, which had won them all these as prizes!

Garlic

Garlic was certainly used in ancient civilizations, mainly by the peasant class. Early priests considered it unclean and sometimes associated it with witches, but by the Middle Ages it was considered a good defence against evil, werewolves, vampires and witches and even became a good luck charm. The Indians in Bolivia still carry a piece for luck when bull-fighting.

In Roman times, criminals were given garlic to purify them of their crimes and it was given to soldiers to give them courage and to labourers to make them strong. Pliny, the famous Roman historian, claimed that garlic was so good that the very smell drove away 'serpents and scorpions.'

In the thirteenth century, a very popular sauce of mustard consistency was made from garlic, almonds, and breadcrumbs crushed together and bound with a little broth, another was onions, garlic, celery and cheese pounded with a pestle and mortar; but by the sixteenth century these were considered only fit for the peasant class.

In France, way back in 1553, the infant who became king was said to have had his lips 'rubbed with garlic' and 'moistened with red wine' at birth and was thus said to have been given the atrributes of a true gourmet.

Wild Garlic

Wild garlic grows prolifically in hedgerows and woodlands, along with primroses and bluebells, and makes a very pretty sight indeed. Walking through a garlic wood is very pungent and appetite-giving to those who like it, though its only culinary use is from the leaves which can be chopped and added to a green salad. The clusters of white, daisy-like flowers are pretty but should be used sparingly in a flower arrangement, if the smell is not to dominate everything else. Wild garlic has innumerable names in Britain, including the following: common or wood garlic, gipsy chipples, onion flowers, ransons, stink plant, snake flower, devil's posy, iron flower, and stinking Jenny.

Chives

The name, chives, is thought to be derived from the Greek for 'rush-leek'; the present name though comes from the French *cive* which means version of onion.

Spring onions

Frequently referred to, especially in the north of England, as 'scallions' or 'Scally onions.'

Remedies

Old cookery and medical books reveal that in a way the onion family was almost the family doctor for it seems there was no end to its ability to cure the most diverse illnesses. Here are just a few 'cures' I have found during my fascinating delving into the history of the onion and its near relations. I cannot however claim to have tried them or be so prophetic about them as our forebears.

Onions

Onions are a recommended cure for insomnia, eaten either raw or lightly stewed, said to be due to the soporific powers of the onion's natural oils.

One suggestion, that 'two or three onions eaten before retiring work like magic for those who cannot sleep,' must I feel be meant only for those sleeping alone, or the partner is likely to be kept awake!

A further potent brew is for 2–3 shredded onions to be cooked in stock until tender, then with the addition of lemon juice, a knob of butter, seasoning and enough water to thin to soup consistency, it should be boiled for 10 minutes. It should be stored in a screw top jar in a refrigerator and a spoonful or two taken before retiring.

For those with a sore throat, particularly with a hoarse voice, onions boiled in molasses are said to do the trick. There are many references to eating a raw onion as defence against catching a cold, aiding digestion, keeping vampires and evil spirits at bay and someone claims that its powers reduce the cholesterol level, which is at least topical if unproven, like all the other claims. An old proverb declared that 'onions make a man wink, drink and stink,' and it is thought that a lot of onion or garlic eaten raw eventually exudes through the pores of one's skin. An old wives' tale, but a friend living in Paris declared it still to be true if one travelled on the Metro in the rush hour! The antidote to smelly hands and breath after preparing or eating onions is to rub the hands with celery or parsley and to eat parsley or drink a cup of strong black coffee.

Interesting, since as a stimulant the coffee should keep you awake – and we started by suggesting that raw onion was a cure for insomnia!!

Leeks

Leeks are particularly recommended as a cure for those suffering from piles, as was revealed in one old book.

Emperor Nero is said to have eaten leeks for several days each month to clear his voice and the Italians declare it to be good for clear operatic singing.

Chives

Chives are said to have been used in China 2,000 years ago as an antidote to poisoning and a remedy for bleeding. As they are rich in an oil containing sulphur (in common with the rest of the onion family), they could be considered an antiseptic so there is some reasoning behind this claim.

Garlic

As garlic is used so sparingly in cooking it does not add a great many nutrients to our diet, but that does not stop its having been claimed for centuries to have health-giving properties. It is said that chewing a clove of garlic helps to cure colds, coughs, pulmonary congestion and recent claims have been made that it lowers our cholesterol level. It is also said to be good used externally for such things as abscesses and earache; it is certainly recorded as being used as an antiseptic as recently as the 1914–18 war.

In Southern Europe it is still considered a digestive stimulant, where appetites are jaded by the heat. In Anglo-Saxon times it featured widely for medicinal purposes, for example for curing a stye in the eye, as a poultice for swelling and as effective against venomous bites, and in a drink against 'demonic' temptations.

Claims that it is good for the complexion do not state whether by internal or external use – if the latter one can only think that the beauty is admired from a distance!

Modern Nutrition

The previous sections have already highlighted the health-giving properties attributed to the onion family. Here is a modern comparative analysis for those who are interested.

Garlic is not included as it is used so sparingly in cooking and chives would read much as spring onions.

Comparison of nutritive value of 25 g/ 1 oz different onions

	Leeks	*Raw Onion*	*Boiled Onion*	*Fried Onion*	*Spring Onions*
Calories	7	7	4	101	10
Protein – g	0.5	0.3	0.2	0.5	0.3
Fat – g	none	none	none	9.5	none
Carbohydrate – g	1.3	1.5	0.8	2.9	2.4
Calcium – mg	17.2	8.9	6.9	17.4	38.4
Iron – mg	0.57	0.09	0.07	0.17	0.35
Vitamin A	none	none	none	none	trace
Vitamin D	none	none	none	none	none
Thiamin – mg	0.02	0.01	trace	none	none
Riboflavin – mg	0.01	0.01	0.01	0.01	none
Vitamin C – mg	4.3	3	2	2	7

How to Grow Your Own

There are many reasons why one should attempt to grow all, or at least some, of the onions described in this brief chapter. For example they are:

1. Easy and fun to grow.
2. Rewarding and inexpensive to cultivate.
3. Take up little room in the small garden.
4. Store well and easily for all year round eating.

I have only attempted to excite you with a brief insight into growing in your own garden, for this is really a book about eating onions and there are lots of good gardening books which will give the enthusiast every possible detail.

CHIVES – Allium schoenoprasum

These are particularly easy to grow, needing a fairly good garden soil and a sunny or semi-shaded position in the garden. As they are also quite decorative, they can happily be grown in the flower border, or make a useful and attractive edging to the vegetable plot. For the 'no garden' household, they grow well in a window-box or patio pot and the purply pin-cushion flower heads, which should be cut anyway to promote growth, are pretty in flower arrangements and posies, but do not overdo them. They are in season outdoors from early spring until late autumn and a winter supply can be obtained by growing them indoors in a pot on the kitchen window-sill.

TO GROW FROM SEED

Sow seeds three or four together at about 30 cm intervals and 5 mm deep. Thin out the weakest of the seedlings and harvest any time from March to October from outdoor plants.

TO GROW FROM PLANTS

The local nursery, market or good neighbour may well be a source of ready-grown roots of chives, which will soon grow large enough to be divided yourself, to produce further plants. Divide in September/October and plant about 30 cm apart.

It is also recommended that established plants are dug up, divided and re-planted every three years.

Note
It is said to improve the growth and flavour of carrots if chives are planted nearby and, joy of joys, they are also said to control black spot in roses if planted underneath them!

ONIONS – Allium cepa

Main crop onions need full sun. Sow from mid-February to the end of March thinly in rows 30 cm apart. Thin to 5 cm, then 10 cm apart. Use thinnings as spring salad onions. Plant onion sets (small dry bulbs) in March/April, 15 cm apart, in rows 30 cm apart, such that only the neck of the bulb is above soil level. Firm bulbs into the soil as they grow. When leaves start to yellow, bend leaves over at the necks of the bulbs so that foliage dries off. When bulb skin yellows, lift with a fork and leave on ground surface to dry and ripen. What is important is that they are removed from the soil before the dampness of autumn evenings adversely affects their storage time, so no later than September, earlier if possible. Store in ropes (see diagram) or boxes or string bags in a cool, dry place.

LEEKS – Allium porrum

Leeks will grow in even the coldest garden, provided there is deeply-dug and well-drained soil.

Sow seeds in shallow drills from March until May for continuity.

Lift the seedlings from June to the end of July when about 20 cm high and trim tops of foliage to promote good root growth. Plant with a dibber in holes 1.5 cm deep, 15 cm apart and 40 cm between rows, fill the holes with water and do not refill with soil. This produces good short thick leeks, for longer well-blanched stems grow in trenches, earthing up to the base of the leaves in September/October.

Keep the rows well weeded and well watered during sunny spells. Lift the leeks as required. They are generally best left in the ground to store as growth through the winter months will only be slow.

They are available in 'long-shanked' or 'short thick' varieties, and your own personal choice will decide which you can buy from your seed catalogue.

SHALLOTS – Allium ascalonicum

Choose an open sunny position, with well-drained soil. Plant the sets in March/April, setting the bulbs 25 cm apart in rows 40 cm apart, the tips of the bulbs being level with the surface of the soil. Control weed growth around the bulbs and as foliage yellows loosen soil from the base of the clumps. About mid-July, as the foliage dies, lift the clumps and leave on the ground surface to dry and ripen. Store in boxes in a cool, dry, frost-free place. Keep a few bulbs for next year's crop.

Note
Shallots may be grown from seeds sown in March, but the bulbs should not be kept for next year's crop, as these tend to bolt and will probably run to seed.

SPRING ONIONS – Allium cepa

For spring onions to be ready to herald the spring, sow seeds thinly in 12 mm drills from July until early September. To have a ready supply through the summer and early autumn, sow each month from March to July. Best eaten when the plant is about 15 cm high. The variety 'White Lisbon' is a good quick-growing one.

Thinnings from 'main crop onion' may be used as spring salad onions.

Note
The *Welsh Onion – Allium fistulonum* – is a perennial which grows to about 30 cm and looks almost like a bunch of spring onions growing together. The thick shoots (there are no bulbs, as such) can be used in place of spring onions and the leaves the same way as chives. Sow as for main crop onions early to late spring in their permanent place in the garden. Thin to give about 25 cm space between each plant; divide clumps every three years.

GARLIC – Allium sativum

Garlic is best grown in a light, well-manured soil in a sunny position.

Use a single clove of garlic, from last year's crop, either home-grown, from the nursery man, the seed catalogue, or even the local delicatessen and plant the pointed end upwards just under the soil about 15 cm apart in February-March. Allow 30 cm between rows.

As there are about a dozen cloves to each garlic bulb, one separated bulb will give you approximately 144 cloves (12x12) and only you will know if that's enough for your cooking requirements. The recipe section may convince you that, perhaps, yet another divided bulb may prove worthwhile!

As the foliage dies down in late August, gently lift the plants from the ground to avoid damaging the bulbs. Allow to dry thoroughly in the sun, then store in a cool dry place. Reserve one or two bulbs for next year's crop.

Legend has it that it will cure peach tree curl if planted beneath peach trees, and also enhance the perfume if grown near them.

The French, who use and therefore buy a good deal more garlic than we do in the UK, can purchase it in a small string (like onions, see diagram page 21) or gathered together in a 'posy' shape rather like a bunch of grapes and often called a grap.

Author's note

The aim of this book is to encourage people to grow and eat the fresh vegetable or herb if possible, but the author does accept that useful store-cupboard standbys are dried onion flakes, onion salt, garlic salt and garlic powder. The flavours are different from using the fresh, but they are certainly recommended if fresh are not available. Always follow manufacturers' recommendations for use, as strengths often vary.

The storage life of these prepared products is as follows:

Onion flakes	– 6 months
Onion salt Garlic salt Garlic powder	– up to 12 months

These recommendations are the optimum times for the products to remain in prime condition and to retain their full flavours. They will still be usable after this time but the strength of flavour will gradually decrease, eventually to nil. The latter three last that much longer because the usual screw top containers are more airtight.

How to Store

This section explains how to store the fresh vegetable for out-of-season eating either by keeping them in a cool dry place, or preparing them ready for cooking and then storing in the freezer.

Storing recommendations

Onions, *shallots* and *garlic* keep well in a cool dry place, either spread out on trays or strung. The diagram below shows how to store by stringing, which is most easily done on a piece of thin rope with the withered tops of the onion left long to twist and tie around the rope. Alternatively, they may be hung, again in a cool dry place, in bags of string or nylon netting, which is probably the better method for the small shallots.

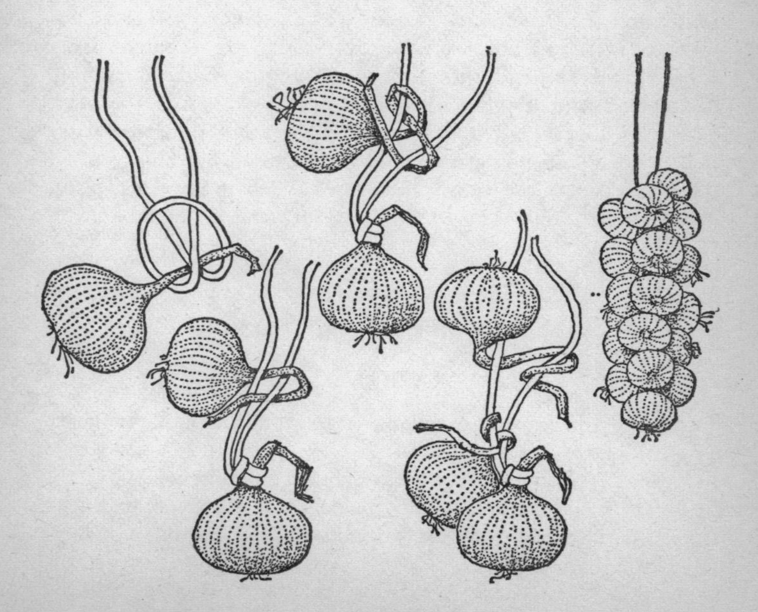

Leeks which grow well during the winter months can be left in the ground and lifted as required; alternatively they freeze well (see page 23).

Chives – With careful sowing this herb can be provided fresh throughout most of the year (see page 17), but can also be frozen very successfully (see page 23).

Spring Onions – Again careful sowing can produce a crop from early summer to late autumn and there is no satisfactory way of storing without losing their fresh taste.

Onion rings – Sometimes people find it useful to have ready prepared onion rings for soups, stews, etc., and those without a freezer may like to try the following methods for drying.

Peel and slice the onion (see page 25) and push through to make the rings, using the few inner circles for cooking fresh straight away. Blanch the onion rings in boiling water for 30 seconds, rinse in cold water, drain and dab dry on absorbent kitchen paper; alternatively, cook the onion rings in a heavy-based saucepan, continually stirring gently until they have softened, adding a tablespoon of salt and a teaspoon of sugar to a little water for every 1 kg/2 lb of onions. After either of these methods, spread the onion rings in single layers on to baking sheets and dry off in a very cool oven, 65°C, 150°F, Gas Mark ¼, with the door slightly open for about 3 hours until the rings are dry and crisp. The salt and sugar method will dry more quickly.

Leave to cool before packing in storage jars kept in a cool, dry place. Reconstitute the onions by placing in warm water for 30 seconds.

Storing in the home freezer

ONIONS

To select: Crisp, firm, fresh onions, large for slicing and chopping, and small button.

To prepare: Peel, slice, chop, or leave button onions whole.

To blanch: Chopped onions pack unblanched; sliced onion rings, floured and blanched in oil for 3 minutes; whole onions in boiling water for 4 minutes.

To freeze and pack: Cool quickly and pack all the above in small

quantities in heavy gauge wrapping materials to prevent odour transfer. No headspace necessary. Seal and label.
Storage life: Unblanched stew pack and fried onions up to 3 months; other onions 6 months.
To thaw: Cook from frozen.
To cook: Whole onions 5–10 minutes in boiling water; floured rings deep fat fry for 2–3 minutes.
To use: Soups, stews, casseroles, sauces; made-up dishes containing onion freeze well; also use for French onion soup, onion sauce, etc.
Recommended varieties for home-freezing: Ailsa Craig, Bedfordshire Champion, Stuttgarter Giant.

SHALLOTS

To freeze: See ONIONS (above)
Recommended varieties for home-freezing: Red Dutch, Yellow Dutch.

LEEKS

To select: Young, clean leeks.
To prepare: Cut off excess green and root; easier to be sure of removal of grit if sliced.
To blanch: Boiling water for 1 minute.
To freeze and pack: Cool quickly and pack in amounts suitable to your requirements in good quality containers to prevent odour transfer. No headspace necessary. Seal and label.
Storage time: 6 months.
To thaw: Cook from frozen.
To cook: Boiling water 5–10 minutes.
To use: Soups, stews and casseroles.
Recommended varieties for home-freezing: The Lyon, Musselburgh, Walton Mammoth, Prizetaker.

CHIVES

To freeze: Gather together a bunch of chives, trim to equal lengths and wrap securely to form a thick stick. Remove from the freezer for use by slicing a few from the end with a sharp knife or scissors, returning the remainder to the freezer storage. May also be chopped and frozen.

SPRING ONIONS

No point in freezing, as crispness is lost during storage.

GARLIC

No point in storing garlic in the freezer, as it stores perfectly well by just leaving to dry.

Its strong pungent smell could well affect the flavour of more delicate items in the freezer if packaging is not first-class. Use garlic sparingly in cooked dishes, as the flavour intensifies during freezer storage.

Preparation and Basic Cooking

It is only when you see people prepare onions or leeks, etc. that you realize many people do not know the correct way, which once shown is always the easiest and most effective. I hope these diagrams and information will mean easier preparation and less waste for you in the future.

Sometimes cookery writers (me included) are so keen to tell you about the recipes they forget not everyone knows the usual ways in which a basic ingredient is prepared, so I have included them all for good measure. To be really up-to-date, how to cook them in the slow cooker, the pressure cooker and the microwave oven have also been included.

Basic cooking methods

ONIONS

Preparation
Remove the outer dry skins and trim at both ends, leave enough at the root end to keep the onion together, either for cooking whole or when slicing or chopping. Wash in cold water.

Sliced onions and onion rings
With the prepared onion on its side, cut through from the neck to root end in the desired thickness, finally discarding the thin root end slice.

Push through each slice to separate for onion rings.

Chopped onions
Chefs have their own way of chopping onions which requires a very sharp knife, practice and dexterity. For the home cook the safest way is to first cut the onion in half from neck to root.

With the flat cut surface on the chopping board, slice through vertically from neck to root, half turn the onion and slice vertically again. The thinner the slice the finer the chopped result.

Note
Use discarded root ends to flavour stock, or in soup making.

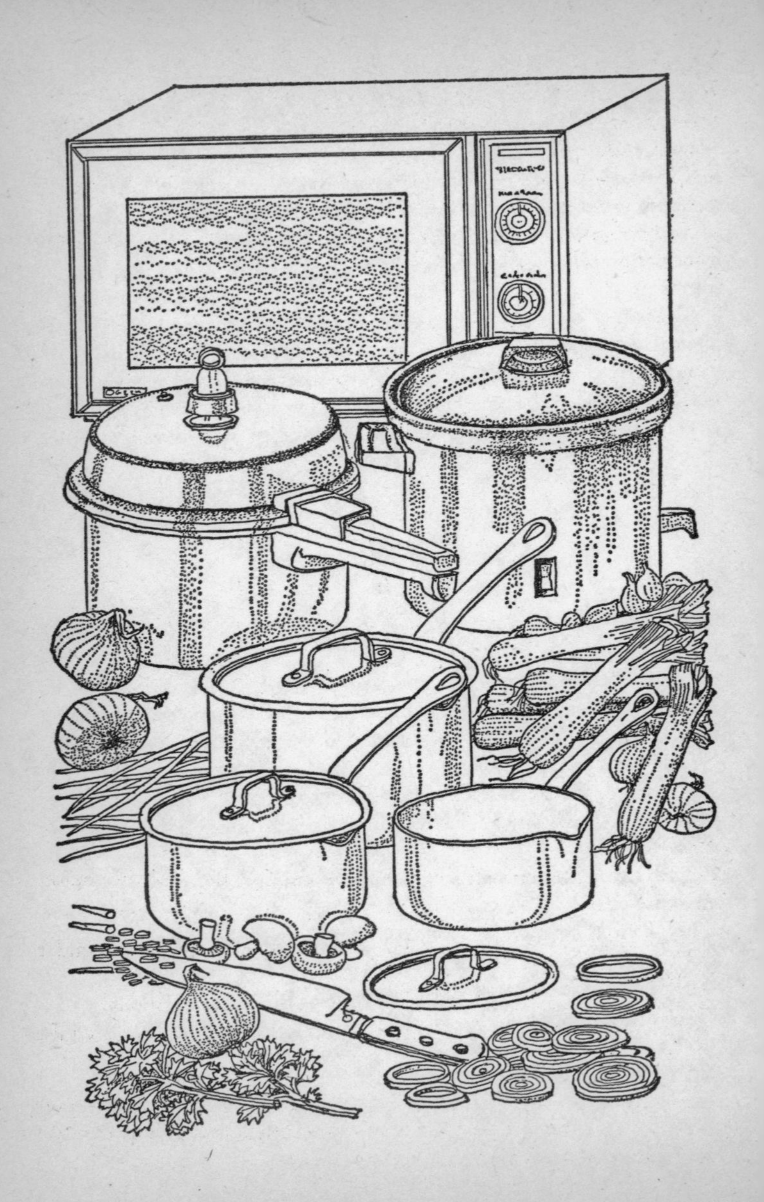

Utensils
A good sharp cook's knife with a heel should be used for the above methods. A patent hand chopper designed for the purpose is on the market and the electrically operated slicer attachment to food mixers and the new food processor make very light work of this job, particularly if several kilograms are being done.

A chopping board kept especially for onions is a good idea to prevent flavour transfer.

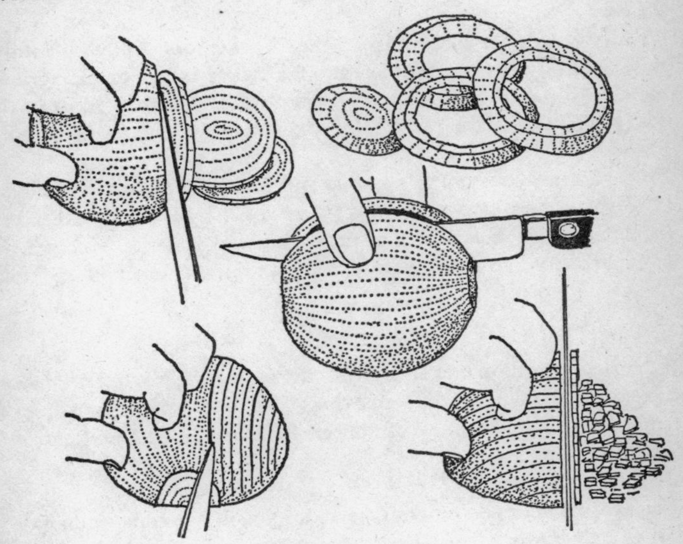

Note
There are all kinds of recommendations for the 'tearful' onion chopper. These are some of them:

1. Do as much of the job with your hands and the onion under water as possible.
2. Hold a crust of bread between your teeth, whilst chopping.
3. Hold the handle of a wooden spoon between your teeth, whilst chopping.

These latter two are, I am sure, more to make you concentrate on holding the crust or handle than for any other reason, but they do work for many people.

Cooking the onion

To boil

Place the prepared onions in boiling salted water and simmer gently until tender.

Large whole onions	50–60 minutes
Small whole onions	20–30 minutes
Chopped onions	5–10 minutes

To bake

Usually onions are sliced into a greased ovenproof dish with a little milk to barely cover, seasoning and a knob of butter or margarine. Cover with a lid or foil and bake in a moderate oven 160–180°C, 325–350°F, Gas Mark 3–4 for approximately 45 minutes to 1 hour.

To roast

Toss whole peeled onions in hot fat and roast near the top of a moderately hot oven 190–200°C, 375–400°F, Gas Mark 5–6, either on their own or around a joint of meat like roast potatoes. Medium to large whole onions would take between 45 minutes to 1 hour to cook through.

Note

If roasting the onion separately from the meat, etc., it is not necessary to remove so many of the outer skins, as the outer layer usually becomes tough and leathery during cooking and is discarded anway, before serving.

To fry or sauté

Shallow fried chopped onions take about 5–6 minutes, depending on how finely chopped and how soft or browned a cooked onion is desired.

Either cook fairly quickly in hot fat or oil, continually stirring in the frying pan to give a stronger flavour and richer colour to sauces, gravies, etc., or fry gently to prevent browning, particularly for light-coloured and delicately flavoured dishes.

Deep frying is usually reserved for onion rings, which may be prepared by any of the following three ways before cooking in hot fat or oil until crisp and golden brown:

1. Toss the onion rings in seasoned flour and fry.
2. Dip the onion rings in milk, then in seasoned flour and fry.
3. Dip the onion rings in batter and fry.

Cooking takes about 3–5 minutes, depending on the thickness of the onion rings, and the number being cooked together. Always drain on absorbent kitchen paper.

Note

The fried onion is an ingredient of a great many recipes in this book and the frying process extracts the onion flavour, which enhances the whole dish. If the onion is fried with other ingredients of the dish at the same time (i.e. garlic, tomatoes) it has the effect of steaming rather than true frying and reduces the aroma of the onion.

The French like the trio combination of onions, shallots and garlic for flavouring casseroles – fry all together in olive oil, but do not brown.

Flavouring

Use a whole onion to stuff the inside of poultry, instead of stuffing.

Use a whole onion studded with cloves for flavouring soups (particularly lentil and pea), also for boiling bacon and ham joints.

Onion juice

Juice scraped with a teaspoon from the centre of a halved onion.

LEEKS

Preparation

Market or home-grown leeks need careful washing to ensure no grit is trapped within the folds of the leaves. Young, forced, pre-packed leeks do not need the same careful inspection.

Remove any badly damaged leaves, trim close to the root end to keep the leek intact. Trim down the upper leaves to the level at which the green part begins to separate. *Do not discard* these trimmings, which make excellent soup.

Leeks may be left whole (good for young ones), cut into about 5–7-cm/2–3-inch pieces, or sliced into about 5–10-mm/$\frac{1}{4}$–$\frac{1}{2}$-inch slices. The cooking time will obviously vary with the size. Some large leeks of which it is difficult to ensure thorough inside cleaning are best slit lengthways.

Cooking the leek

To boil

Use a minimum of salted water and a lidded saucepan. Young whole and large pieces take about 15–20 minutes, thin slices and rings between 5–10 minutes. Whole leeks and thick pieces tend to retain a good deal of water, so drain well, pressing water gently from the leeks, or return to the heat for a few seconds after draining to steam-off any excess water.

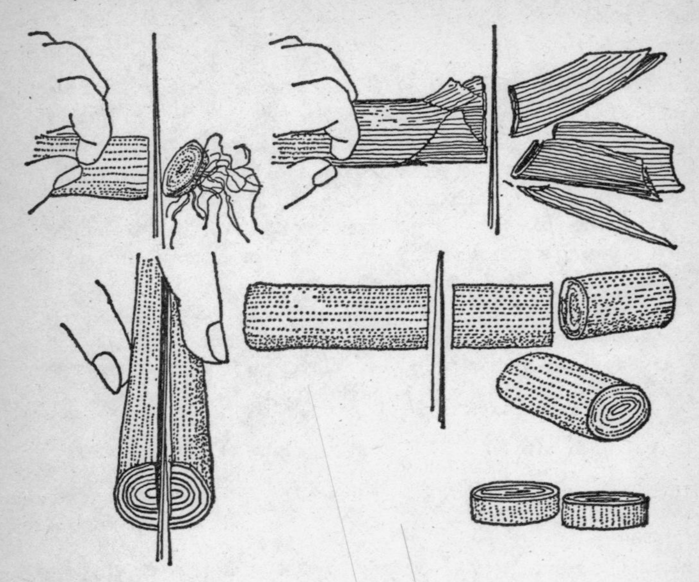

Note
If the leeks are not drained well and are served in a sauce, they tend to 'weep' and thus dilute the sauce.

To pan-fry
Melt butter in a pan with a close-fitting lid, add thinly sliced leeks plus seasoning and cook covered (*without any water*) for about 5 minutes, shaking or stirring frequently. Use 40 g/1½ oz butter to 450 g /1 lb leeks.

Leeks do not lend themselves so readily to the roasting and frying methods given previously for onions; they can however be baked using the same onion method.

Finely shredded young leeks can also be added to salads.

Note
Mrs Beeton says, 'Re-boil leeks in 3 or 4 waters, then stew gently in milk until tender. Drain well, quarter and serve on hot, buttered toast. Almost as delicate as asparagus.'

SHALLOTS

Generally speaking, these small onions are used in this country mainly for pickling (see page 187), though they are used a lot in French cooking where their flavour, although milder than the big onion, is often preferred, particularly for delicately flavoured recipes. They are particularly suited to soups, sauces and stock, where they enhance rather than predominate over other flavours.

Preparation

Pull apart, as they grow in bunches, then peel away the skin and top and tail as usual. They are attractive used whole in a casserole or pie; they are a little more time consuming to prepare, of course, but frequently worth it.

CHIVES

Chives, which are easy to grow (see page 17), can be used when just a hint of 'oniony' flavour is needed in a recipe, but are at their best served raw in salads, or mixed with scrambled eggs, mashed potato, cream or cottage cheese and are delicious with tomato in sandwiches and make delicate-flavoured stuffings. They are an essential ingredient of Tartare sauce and are good added to any salad dressing, either oil and vinegar or mayonnaise based.

The easiest preparation method is to gather a bunch together, rinse under cold water and cut through the bunch with a pair of scissors.

Chives added to onions and shallots whilst they are cooking are said to give them a better flavour.

SPRING ONIONS

Rather wasteful and expensive to use in cooking, but invaluable in salads. Prepare by trimming the root and cutting away the green about 5 cm/2 inches above the white. Don't however, throw the green away, but use chopped to flavour soup and stocks.

Spring onions may be used in all the ways listed under **chives.**

GARLIC

Even those professing not to like garlic will often praise the flavour of a dish, not realizing that the hint of garlic has brought out all the flavours to perfection, so for the non-converted, garlic should be used with discretion.

When purchasing garlic, one is buying a whole garlic *bulb* which, with the outer skin peeled away, will give about 12 single cloves and each single clove goes a long way in flavouring dishes either hot or cold. Remove the dry skin from each clove and crush to release the flavour.

Preparation may be with a patent press designed for the purpose, though many cooks claim some of the valuable juices are lost in this way. Alternatively, the clove may be finely chopped or crushed with the point of the knife, or even left whole for casseroles and stews and removed before serving.

Using a clove of garlic to rub around a salad bowl, or to rub over chops and steaks, imparts a delicate but distinctive flavour.

An alternative method for flavouring salads is to rub a thick crust of bread with a cut clove or two of garlic and a sprinkling of salt. Place at the bottom of a salad bowl with the salad on top allowing the flavour to penetrate up before removing it and tossing the salad. The rubbing of the salad bowl with a cut clove only really works on a wooden bowl, so this method is useful for glass, plastic, etc.

One or two single cloves cut into thin strips and then pressed into a joint of beef or lamb, porcupine fashion, truly transforms a simple joint. Remove slivers of garlic before serving.

Garlic flavouring in casseroles, etc., tends to intensify during freezing, so either use slightly less or add when reheating the dish to serve.

Wild garlic leaves, when you can find them, give a delicious tang when chopped into a green salad.

Microwave cooking

Both onions and leeks can be very successfully cooked in a microwave oven. Follow the cooking directions given with your cooker, as many makes vary a little. The following is a useful guide:

		Quantity	*Water*	*Cooking Time*
Onions	– large whole	2	None	6–8 minutes
	– large quartered	450 g/1 lb	None	6–8 minutes
	– small whole	8	None	6–7 minutes
Leeks	– sliced	450 g/1 lb	2 tablespoons	10 minutes

It is recommended that they are cooked in a covered container, or the dish is covered with cling film.

Note
The author has found that chopped onions and a little butter in a shakeable microwave container soften, but do not of course brown, but are quick when a recipe demands this. Timing, of course, varies with the quantity.

Two microwave recipes can be found on page 111–12 and many of the recipes in this book can be adapted by the experienced microwave user.

Slow cooking

Long slow cooking in the stoneware pot of an electric slow cooker produces tasty, succulent food which can be left cooking all day, without risk of drying up or burning. One of the unusual characteristics of slow cooking is that vegetables can take longer to cook than meat. Consequently, onions should be chopped small and, if possible, softened slightly by sautéing before adding to the slow cooker. As there is little loss of steam during cooking, smells are trapped in the slow cooker. This also means that flavours are slightly stronger and onion flavouring may need to be adjusted accordingly.

Pressure cooking

A pressure cooker traps most of the steam which normally escapes from a pan and harnesses it to speed up cooking. The small amount of evaporation means that cooking smells don't escape and flavours are retained. Consequently, smaller amounts of onion are required to add flavouring to dishes. French onion soup can be cooked in 4 minutes and Vichyssoise in 5 minutes. The trivet may be used to raise food above the water during cooking and delicious stuffed onions can be cooked in only 7 minutes.

Appetizers and Starters

I wouldn't like to think these recipes were only considered for the beginning of a meal, for in larger portions or combined with a soup they make meals in themselves; they also make an attractive and very acceptable part of a buffet table.

They had to be categorized in some way, and this seemed logical, but don't miss out on their taste just because 'starters' are not on your menu!

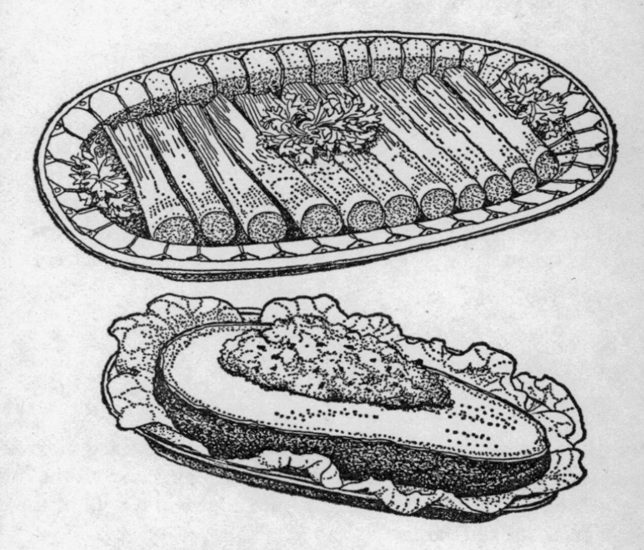

AUBERGINE PÂTÉ

Cooking time 35–45 minutes Serves 4–6

METRIC/IMPERIAL

2 medium aubergines
2½ tablespoons salad oil
100 g/4 oz butter
1 large onion, finely chopped
generous pinch mixed herbs
1 teaspoon lemon juice
seasoning

Wash the aubergines and dry well. Slice them, sprinkle liberally with salt and leave for 15 minutes in a refrigerator, covered with cling film. Heat the oil and half the butter in a frying pan and sauté the onion until soft. Dry off the aubergine slices, add to the onion and cook for 35–45 minutes, stirring the pan frequently, until the vegetables are soft. Add another 25 g/1 oz of the butter, the herbs and lemon juice and place all the ingredients in a liquidizer and blend until smooth. Add the seasoning to taste, using freshly ground black pepper for preference. Pour into a serving dish and chill. When quite cold, melt the remaining 25 g/1 oz of the butter and pour over the pâté to seal.

Will keep well for 4–5 days in a refrigerator.

LIVER SAUSAGE PÂTÉ

Cooking time few minutes Serves 6–8

METRIC/IMPERIAL

3 rashers bacon, finely chopped
3 tablespoons finely chopped spring onion
500 g/18 oz liver sausage
100 g/4 oz butter, softened
2–3 tablespoons dry sherry
seasoning

To garnish
sliced olives
watercress

Fry the bacon gently and when the fat begins to show add the onions and soften slightly. Liquidize the bacon and onion and all the other ingredients in a blender. Pack tightly into a greased mould or tin and chill. Turn out and garnish to serve.

PÂTÉ FOR SPRINGTIME

Cooking time few minutes Serves 4

METRIC/IMPERIAL

3–4 large spring onions, finely chopped
1 large stick celery, finely chopped
1 clove garlic, crushed
100 g/4 oz butter
1 (200-g/7-oz) can tuna fish
2 tablespoons mayonnaise (see page 180)
2 ripe tomatoes, peeled
2 teaspoons lemon juice
4 tablespoons double cream
seasoning

To garnish
slices of lemon
parsley sprigs

Sauté the onions, celery and garlic in the hot butter until soft. Drain the tuna fish and place all the ingredients, except the double cream, in a liquidizer and blend thoroughly. Add the cream and blend for 1 minute. Check seasoning: freshly ground black pepper is best. Place in individual ramekin dishes. Serve well chilled, garnished with slices of lemon and parsley sprigs.

TARAMASALATA 1

Serves 4–6

METRIC/IMPERIAL

1 tablespoon fresh breadcrumbs
225 g/8 oz smoked cod's roe
juice of 1 lemon
2 cloves garlic
1 tablespoon oil

To garnish
slices of lemon
black olives
lettuce

Soak the breadcrumbs in a little water and then squeeze well. Place the cod's roe, lemon juice, breadcrumbs and garlic in a liquidizer and blend together well, adding the oil halfway through blending. Serve individual portions of taramasalata on a lettuce leaf, each garnished with a slice of lemon and a black olive. Serve with brown bread and butter.

TARAMASALATA 2

Serves 6

METRIC/IMPERIAL

50 g/2 oz stale bread
100 g/4 oz fish roe (smoked or not)
1 onion, grated
juice of 2 lemons
300 ml/½ pint olive oil

Soak the bread in water for a few minutes, drain and squeeze out the water.

Pound the fish roe until smooth. Mix together the roe, bread, onion and lemon juice and gradually beat in the oil vigorously.

Alternatively, liquidizing all the ingredients together in a blender makes very light work of preparing this dish. Chill in the refrigerator, before serving with toast.

DANISH MARINATED HERRINGS

Serves 6 (as a starter)

METRIC/IMPERIAL

6 herring fillets
300 ml/½ pint double cream
3 tablespoons wine vinegar
½ tablespoon olive oil
3 small onions, finely chopped
3 black peppercorns
1 apple, peeled, cored and sliced
½ small cooked beetroot, sliced
½ lemon, thinly sliced
2–3 small bay leaves

Wash the herring fillets, dab dry and place in a bowl. Mix all the other ingredients together and pour over the herrings. Cover the bowl and refrigerate for 24 hours, before serving well chilled.

HERBY HERRINGS

Cooking time 10–12 minutes Serves 4

METRIC/IMPERIAL

4 herrings, filleted
seasoning
6–8 tablespoons fresh breadcrumbs or oatmeal
50 g/2 oz margarine

Dressing

150 ml/¼ pint thick mayonnaise (see page 180)
1 tablespoon finely chopped onion
1 tablespoon chopped chives
1 tablespoon finely chopped dill or fennel
2 hard-boiled eggs, chopped
1 tablespoon lemon juice
wedges of lemon to garnish

Season the herrings and lightly coat in the oatmeal or breadcrumbs. Fry the herrings in the margarine for 5–6 minutes on each side. Combine all the ingredients for the dressing and serve separately with the hot cooked herrings, garnishing with the lemon.

PICKLED CURRIED FISH

Cooking time 35 minutes
Oven temperature Moderate 180°C, 350°F, Gas Mark 4

METRIC/IMPERIAL

3.5 kg/8 lb any white fish fillets
salt
8 large onions, sliced
4 tablespoons oil
3½ tablespoons curry powder
1.5 litres/2¾ pints vinegar
1½ tablespoons sugar
¼ teaspoon cayenne pepper
2 teaspoons salt
2 bay leaves

Sprinkle the fish fillets with salt and leave to stand for 2 hours, then bake the fish in a greased ovenproof dish for 30 minutes in a moderate oven.

Fry the onions in the oil until golden brown, add the curry powder, vinegar, sugar, cayenne pepper and salt. Boil together for a few minutes. Pack a layer of fish into an earthenware dish or jar, place a bay leaf on top, pour over the curry/vinegar mixture, continuing layering until all the ingredients are used. Allow to cool and cover with a greaseproof paper cap. Chill for at least 24 hours before eating.

Keep in the refrigerator or a cool place, where the fish will last for several weeks.

PRAWNS IN GARLIC MAYONNAISE

Serves 4

METRIC/IMPERIAL

50 g/2 oz peeled prawns
4 tablespoons cooked rice
1 tablespoon sultanas
1 tablespoon chopped nuts
300 ml/½ pint Garlic mayonnaise (see page 181)

Combine the first four ingredients and toss in the mayonnaise.

Serve on a lettuce leaf, garnished with a slice of lemon and a sprig of parsley.

AVOCADO APPETISER

Serves 4

METRIC/IMPERIAL

4 ripe avocado pears
juice of 1 lemon
1 clove garlic, crushed
4 tomatoes, peeled and chopped
½ large Spanish onion, finely chopped
2 tablespoons finely chopped celery
2 tablespoons finely chopped green pepper
1 tablespoon finely chopped parsley
2–4 tablespoons olive oil
salt
freshly ground black pepper

Peel and mash the avocados. Add the lemon juice, garlic, tomatoes, onion, celery and green pepper. Stir in the parsley, olive oil and seasoning to taste. Chill quickly, but serve before the avocados begin to turn brown.

CHIVE STUFFED AVOCADOS

Serves 4

METRIC/IMPERIAL

1 medium onion, finely chopped
½ green pepper, seeded and chopped
40 g/1½ oz walnuts, chopped
1 teaspoon chopped parsley
1 tablespoon chopped chives
pinch nutmeg
1 (142-ml/5-fl oz) carton soured cream
2 avocados
seasoning

Combine all the ingredients, except the avocados and season to taste. Cut the avocados in half, remove the stones and fill with the mixture. Serve well chilled, as soon as possible.

STUFFED TOMATOES

Cooking time 25 minutes
Oven temperature Moderate 180°C, 350°F, Gas Mark 4
Serves 8 (as a starter) 4 (as an accompanying vegetable)

METRIC/IMPERIAL

8 large tomatoes
1 tablespoon oil
25 g/1 oz butter
1 clove garlic, crushed
1 large onion, finely chopped
2 sticks celery, finely chopped
100 g/4 oz streaky bacon, finely chopped
50 g/2 oz fresh white breadcrumbs
1 teaspoon oregano
4 tablespoons chopped parsley
seasoning
25 g/1 oz cheese, grated

Slice the tops from the tomatoes, scoop out the insides and reserve both. Heat the oil and butter together, add the garlic, onion, celery, bacon and tomato pulp and cook gently for 5 minutes. Remove from the heat and mix in the breadcrumbs, seasoning and herbs. Fill the tomatoes well with the mixture, sprinkle with cheese and replace the tomato tops. Place in a greased ovenproof dish and bake, covered, until the tomatoes are cooked, about 20 minutes. Serve hot or cold.

TUNISIAN VEGETABLES

Cooking time 1 hour 10 minutes Oven temperature Moderately hot 190°c, 375°F, Gas Mark 5 Serves 4

METRIC/IMPERIAL

3 onions, sliced finely
2 tablespoons oil
675 g/1½ lb tomatoes, peeled and chopped
3 green peppers, seeded and sliced
salt
pinch cayenne pepper
pinch sugar
4 eggs

Sauté the onions in the oil until softened, add the tomatoes and peppers and seasoning. Cover the pan and allow to simmer gently for one hour, removing the lid for the last five minutes to allow some of the liquid to evaporate.

Butter four small ovenproof dishes and divide the vegetable mixture between them. Make a slight depression in each and break an egg into each. Bake in a moderately hot oven until the eggs are set, about 10 minutes.

BARBADOS STARTER

Cooking Time 40 minutes Serves 4–6

METRIC/IMPERIAL

2 large onions
450 g/1 lb mushrooms
50 g/2 oz butter
seasoning
2 teaspoons Angostura bitters
300 ml/½ pint double (or soured) cream
40g/1½ oz blanched almonds, toasted
a little chopped parsley to garnish

Slice the onions and mushrooms and sauté the onions first until tender but not brown. Add the mushrooms and cook for a further 3–4 minutes, season and get the pan very hot before pouring in the Angostura bitters, then set alight, allowing the flames to burn out. Pour in the cream, heat through gently and divide into individual warmed serving dishes. Sprinkle the tops with the almonds and parsley.

COURGETTES AND ONION STARTER

Cooking time 5–10 minutes Serves 4

METRIC/IMPERIAL

4 courgettes
2 onions
1 clove garlic, crushed
50 g/2 oz butter
6 tablespoons chicken stock
seasoning

Wash and slice the courgettes. Slice the onions finely and mix with the garlic. Fry the onions in the butter until softened, add the courgettes, seasoning and stock and simmer gently until all the stock is absorbed, when the courgettes will be cooked but still firm.

Serve garnished with chopped parsley and a slice of hot toast.

ONION STARTER FROM MONACO

Cooking time 1 hour Serves 4

METRIC/IMPERIAL

1 carrot, coarsely chopped
2 tablespoons olive oil
450 g/1 lb small onions or shallots, peeled
250 ml/8 fl oz water
4 tablespoons dry white wine
2 tablespoons lemon juice
25 g/1 oz sultanas
1 tablespoon tomato purée
1 bay leaf
generous pinch thyme
salt
freshly ground black pepper
cayenne
olive oil
finely chopped parsley to garnish

Sauté the carrot in olive oil until it softens and is golden. Add all the ingredients (except the last two), seasoning to suit personal taste. Simmer for about an hour, until the onions are tender. Chill in the refrigerator and before serving, correct seasoning. Add just a little olive oil and garnish with parsley.

LEEK SALAD STARTER

Cooking time 5–10 minutes Serves 6–8

METRIC/IMPERIAL

150 ml/¼ pint French dressing (see page 181)	8–12 young leeks
	chopped parsley to garnish

Preferably make up the French dressing with lemon juice, instead of vinegar. Trim, clean and cook the leeks until they are just tender. Drain thoroughly, pressing out all the water. Cool, pour over the dressing, garnish with the parsley and serve. This salad may also be served to accompany a main course.

PEKING LEEKS

Cooking time 5–8 minutes Serves 4

METRIC/IMPERIAL

1 kg/2 lb young leeks, trimmed and washed well	1 tablespoon soy sauce
4 tablespoons vinegar	1 tablespoon honey
1 tablespoon oil	1 tablespoon demerara sugar
2 tablespoons tomato ketchup	salt
	50 g/2 oz sultanas

Trim the root end of the long thin leeks carefully, so that the leaves are held together well.

Simmer the leeks in a shallow pan of boiling water for 5–8 minutes, until tender. Drain well and place on a serving dish. Mix all the ingredients, except the sultanas, together and stir over a low heat until the sugar and honey have dissolved. Remove from the heat and add the sultanas. Pour over the leeks and chill for at least an hour before serving.

BACON AND BANANA KEBABS

Cooking time 15 minutes Serves 4

METRIC/IMPERIAL

8 shallots
1 small red pepper, seeded and cut into 8 pieces
1 tablespoon Worcestershire sauce
juice of 1 lemon
seasoning
150 g/5 oz streaky bacon, with rind removed
4 bananas, cut into 3.5-cm/1½ inch pieces
100 g/4 oz button mushrooms

Prepare the shallots carefully leaving them whole, cook in boiling water for 5 minutes and drain. Blanch the prepared pepper for 1 minute and drain. Mix together the Worcestershire sauce, lemon juice and seasoning. Stretch the rashers of bacon on a board with the back of a knife until they are twice their length, then cut in half. Coat each piece of banana with the Worcestershire sauce mixture and then wrap around with a piece of prepared bacon. Arrange the onions, banana rolls, mushrooms and pepper alternately on 4 skewers. Brush all over with the remaining Worcestershire sauce mixture. Place under a moderately hot grill for 5 minutes, turn over, baste and grill for a further 5 minutes.

Soups

Soups seem to once again be gaining in popularity, perhaps because they are almost in some cases a meal in themselves, perhaps because blenders, pressure cookers, slow-cookers, etc. have all made the making of them so much easier. Perhaps too, home-made soups have been rediscovered because cooks have realized how infinitely superior they are in flavour when compared to the bland sameness of the bought varieties. I hope you enjoy this selection.

CORN CHOWDER

Cooking time 1 hour Serves 6–8

METRIC/IMPERIAL

100 g/4 oz lean streaky bacon, chopped
25 g/1 oz butter
3 large celery sticks, finely chopped
1 large onion, finely chopped
2 tablespoons flour
600 ml/1 pint chicken stock
225 g/8 oz potatoes, peeled and cut into 2.5-cm/1-inch cubes
1 small green pepper, seeded and chopped
1 bay leaf
seasoning
450 ml/¾ pint milk
1 (350-g/12-oz) can sweet corn, drained
150 ml/¼ pint single cream
chopped parsley to garnish

Fry the bacon in the butter in a large saucepan and cook until almost crisp. Add the celery and onion and continue cooking until tender, then add the flour and cook for 1 minute. Gradually add the chicken stock and when it is well-blended add the potatoes, green pepper, bay leaf and seasoning. Bring to the boil and simmer for about 20 minutes, until the vegetables are tender. Add the milk and sweet corn and reheat for a further 30 minutes, but do not allow to boil. Serve with a swirl of cream on each individual dish and a sprinkling of chopped parsley.

ONION SOUP – FRENCH STYLE

Cooking time 30–45 minutes Serves 4

METRIC/IMPERIAL

450 g/1 lb onions, chopped
50 g/2 oz margarine
15 g/½ oz flour
1 litre/1¾ pints stock, using 3 beef cubes
1 teaspoon Worcestershire sauce
seasoning
4 slices French bread
50 g/2 Cheddar cheese, grated

Sauté the onions in the margarine until brown, about 12–15 minutes. Add the flour and stock and gently whisk until the mixture comes to the boil. Simmer for 20–30 minutes. Add the Worcestershire sauce and seasoning to taste. Sprinkle each slice of French bread with grated cheese and brown under the grill. Float each on an individual bowl of soup, before serving.

CREAM OF ONION SOUP

Cooking time 50 minutes Serves 4–6

METRIC/IMPERIAL

450 g/1 lb onions, finely sliced
50 g/2 oz butter
2 tablespoons flour
1 litre/1¾ pints chicken stock
1½ teaspoons salt
freshly milled pepper
4 tablespoons dry white wine
4 tablespoons double cream
chopped chives to garnish

Sauté the onions in the butter until soft, about 5–10 minutes. Stir in the flour and cook for a further 2 minutes. Gradually add the stock and simmer for 25 minutes. Liquidize in a blender, season to taste, add the wine and cream and simmer for 10 minutes, without allowing the soup to boil. Serve garnished with chopped chives.

SOUFFLÉ ONION SOUP

Cooking time 10 minutes Serves 6
Oven temperature Hot 230°C, 450°F, Gas Mark 8

METRIC/IMPERIAL

6 tablespoons grated cheese
450 ml/¾ pint Béchamel sauce (see page 174)
2 egg whites, stiffly beaten
1.4 litres/2½ pints French Onion soup (see page 47)
slices French bread

Add the cheese to the Béchamel sauce, allow to cool, then fold in the stiffly beaten egg whites. Top the onion soup with the bread in the normal way, but spoon the cheese soufflé mixture on top instead of grated cheese. Bake in a hot oven for 8–10 minutes, until risen and golden brown. Serve at once.

COCK-A-LEEKIE SOUP

Cooking time 2–2½ hours Serves 4–6

METRIC/IMPERIAL

4 leeks
3 chicken joints
50 g/2 oz pearl barley
1.4 litres/2½ pints water
1 teaspoon salt
freshly ground pepper
1 bay leaf

Slice the leeks into 1 cm/½-inch rings. Put all the ingredients into a heavy-based pan and bring to the boil. Simmer until the chicken is cooked, then remove from the heat and cool. Take out the chicken portions and discard the skin and bones. Chop the chicken flesh into small pieces. Remove any fat from the cold soup. Return the chicken, bring to the boil and serve.

CURRIED APPLE SOUP

Cooking Time 10–15 minutes Serves 4

METRIC/IMPERIAL

1 onion, chopped
1 tablespoon curry powder
25 g/1 oz butter
1 tablespoon cornflour
150 ml/¼ pint apple purée
600 ml/1 pint chicken stock
2 egg yolks
150 ml/¼ pint cream
1 tablespoon lemon juice
seasoning
1 eating apple, peeled, cored and diced, tossed in lemon juice

Fry the onion and curry powder in the butter. Mix the cornflour with a little water. Combine the onion, apple purée, chicken stock and the cornflour mixture and bring to the boil. Simmer for 6–7 minutes. Beat the egg yolks into the cream, stir into the apple mixture with the lemon juice and seasoning and cook very gently for about 2 minutes. Remove the mixture from the heat, sieve and chill. Serve pieces of diced apple with each dish of soup.

AVOCADO VICHYSSOISE

Cooking time 25 minutes Serves 6

METRIC/IMPERIAL

450 g/1 lb potatoes, sliced
2 leeks (white part only), finely sliced
1 onion, finely sliced
750 ml/1¼ pints chicken stock
300 ml/½ pint single cream
1 large avocado, chopped into small pieces
salt
freshly ground pepper
3 tablespoons dry sherry

Cook the potatoes, leeks and onion in the chicken stock until tender; sieve or liquidize in a blender. Stir in the cream and avocado pieces and season to taste. Stir in the sherry and either chill or reheat, without boiling.

ONION AND GREEN PEPPER SOUP

Cooking time 20–25 minutes Serves 4–6

METRIC/IMPERIAL

2 large onions, finely chopped
1–2 cloves garlic, crushed
2 tablespoons oil
1 large green pepper, seeded and thinly sliced
1 large red pepper, seeded and thinly sliced
900 ml/1½ pints chicken stock
2 large tomatoes, peeled and chopped
50–100 g/2–4 oz mushrooms, sliced
seasoning

To garnish
grated cheese
chopped parsley

Sauté the onions and garlic in the oil, until transparent. Add the peppers and mix for a further few seconds. Add the stock, bring to the boil, then add the tomatoes and mushrooms, simmering gently until the vegetables are just cooked. Season to taste. Garnish with cheese and parsley.

ONION AND PARSNIP SOUP

Cooking time 20 minutes Serves 4

METRIC/IMPERIAL

225 g/8 oz onions, diced
225 g/8 oz parsnips, diced
50 g/2 oz butter
900 ml/1½ pints chicken stock
single cream or top of milk
pinch curry powder
seasoning
40 g/1½ oz walnuts, chopped

Sauté the onions and parsnips in the butter. When they are beginning to brown add the stock and bring to the boil. Simmer for 15–20 minutes. Liquidize in a blender and return the purée to a saucepan with enough single cream to give the correct consistency. Add the curry powder and season to taste. Gently reheat the soup and serve sprinkled with the chopped walnuts.

PEANUT SOUP

Cooking time 45 minutes Serves 4

METRIC/IMPERIAL

225 g/8 oz shelled unsalted peanuts
100 g/4 oz onion, chopped
25 g/1 oz butter
450 ml/¾ pint chicken stock
450 ml/¾ pint milk
pepper
1 tablespoon cream
3 tablespoons sherry
chopped chives to garnish

Blanch to skin the nuts, if necessary. Crush them with a pestle and mortar or in a polythene bag with a rolling pin. Fry the onion in the butter until it is soft but not browned. Add the nuts, stirring continually, then the chicken stock, bring to the boil and simmer for 45 minutes. Liquidize the mixture in a blender. Add the milk, pepper to taste and bring to the boil. Stir in the cream and sherry and serve garnished with the chopped chives.

TOMATO AND ORANGE SOUP

Cooking time 20–30 minutes Serves 4

METRIC/IMPERIAL

1 (794-g/1¾-lb) can tomatoes
1 large onion, chopped
1 carrot, chopped
1 bay leaf
750 ml/1¼ pints chicken stock
15 g/½ oz flour
15 g/½ oz margarine
grated rind and juice of 1 orange
pinch sugar
seasoning
chopped parsley to garnish

Place the tomatoes, onion, carrot, bay leaf and stock in a saucepan and bring to the boil, then simmer for 20–30 minutes. Liquidize in a blender, adding the flour and margarine and orange rind and juice. Place all the soup ingredients together with the sugar and seasoning to taste into a clean saucepan and bring to the boil. Serve with a sprinkling of chopped parsley.

VICHYSSOISE

(Cold cream of leek and potato soup)

Cooking time 25 minutes Serves 6

METRIC/IMPERIAL

4 large potatoes, sliced
4 large leeks, prepared and sliced
600 ml/1 pint chicken stock
600 ml/1 pint milk
300 ml/½ pint single cream
15 g/½ oz butter
2 teaspoons salt
¼ teaspoon pepper

To garnish
4 tablespoons chopped chives
½ teaspoon paprika

Cook the potatoes and leeks in the stock until quite soft (about 20 minutes). Liquidize in a blender, or sieve. Add the milk, cream, butter and seasoning to the purée and reheat gently. Serve either hot or well chilled with a sprinkling of chopped chives and paprika to garnish.

LEEK AND POTATO SOUP

Cooking time 30 minutes Serves 4–6

METRIC/IMPERIAL

3 large leeks
8 large spring onions
50 g/2 oz butter
350 g/12 oz potatoes, diced
900 ml/1½ pints chicken stock
300 ml/½ pint milk
150 ml/¼ pint single cream
seasoning
chopped chives to garnish

Prepare and wash the leeks and spring onions thoroughly, then slice and shred them finely. Sauté the onions and leeks in the butter in a large pan for about 5–10 minutes. Add the potatoes and stock, bring to the boil and simmer for about 20 minutes until the potatoes are cooked. Liquidize in a blender, or sieve, and return to the saucepan, adding the milk and cream. Reheat, but do not boil. Adjust seasoning to taste and garnish with chopped chives.

CARROT SOUP

Cooking time 45 minutes Serves 6

METRIC/IMPERIAL

1 large onion, finely chopped
450 g/1 lb carrots, sliced
50 g/2 oz butter
1 litre/1¾ pints stock
1 teaspoon sugar
¼ teaspoon powdered mace
seasoning
1 teaspoon cornflour
150 ml/¼ pint single cream

To garnish
garlic-flavoured croûtons (see page 139)
1 tablespoon chopped mint

Lightly fry the onion and carrots in the butter in a large saucepan. Add the stock and bring to the boil, then simmer for 30–40 minutes. Liquidize in a blender, or sieve. Return to the saucepan, adding the sugar, mace, seasoning to tast and the cornflour mixed with the cream. Reheat, but do not boil. Serve in soup bowls, garnished with croûtons and chopped mint.

CHEESE AND ONION SOUP

Cooking time 25–30 minutes Serves 4

METRIC/IMPERIAL

1 large onion, finely chopped
2 sticks celery, finely chopped
25 g/1 oz butter
300 ml/½ pint water
600 ml/1 pint milk
1½ tablespoons cornflour
2 tablespoons Worcestershire sauce
150 g/5 oz Cheddar cheese, grated
seasoning

To garnish
chopped parsley
extra 25 g/1 oz mature Cheddar cheese, grated

Sauté the onion and celery in the butter for 5 minutes. Add the water and the milk, bring to the boil and simmer for 20 minutes. Blend the cornflour with the Worcestershire sauce and stir into the soup, bringing to the boil. Add the cheese and reheat, but do not boil. Season to taste and garnish with the chopped parsley and extra grated cheese. Serve with crusty French bread.

CHILLED CUCUMBER AND CHIVE SOUP

Cooking time 10 minutes Serves 4

METRIC/IMPERIAL

1 small onion, chopped
½ cucumber, peeled and diced
15 g/½ oz butter
3 (150-g/5.3-oz) cartons natural yogurt
300 ml/½ pint chicken stock
grated rind and juice of 1 lemon
2 tablespoons chopped chives
seasoning, including freshly ground black pepper

Sauté the onion and cucumber in butter for 8–10 minutes. Cool, add the yoghurt, stock, lemon and chives. Season to taste and serve well chilled.

DIFFERENT TOMATO SOUP

Cooking time 30 minutes Serves 4–5

METRIC/IMPERIAL

2 onions, finely chopped
2 cloves garlic, crushed
40 g/1½ oz butter
20 g/¾ oz flour
300 ml/½ pint tomato juice
300 ml/½ pint fish stock
150 ml/¼ pint orange juice
¼ bottle dry white wine
seasoning
100 g/4 oz prawns, shelled
2 tomatoes, peeled, seeded and chopped
4 tablespoons double cream

To garnish
1 tablespoon chopped parsley
segments from an orange

Sauté the onions and garlic in the butter until they are soft but not brown, stir in the flour and gradually blend in all the liquid ingredients, except the cream. Season to taste. Bring to the boil and simmer for 30 minutes. Add the prawns, tomatoes and cream, reheat but do not boil. Serve garnished with the orange segments and chopped parsley.

COLD SPRING SOUP

Cooking time 10 minutes Serves 4

METRIC/IMPERIAL

4 young carrots, scraped and thinly sliced
4 new potatoes, scraped and cut into 5-mm/¼-inch cubes
50 g/2 oz button mushrooms
225 g/8 oz fresh peas, shelled
4 large spring onions, chopped
300 ml/½ pint chicken stock
300 ml/½ pint milk
2 teaspoons cornflour
150 ml/¼ pint double cream
3 tomatoes, peeled, seeded and chopped
4 teaspoons Worcestershire sauce
chopped chives to garnish

Place all the vegetables, except the tomatoes, in a saucepan with the stock, bring to the boil and then simmer for 10 minutes. Blend a little of the milk with the cornflour, stir it into the saucepan and bring to the boil, stirring until the soup has thickened. Add the remaining milk, the double cream, chopped tomatoes and Worcestershire sauce. Chill well before serving, sprinkled with the chopped chives.

COUNTRY SOUP

Cooking time 1–1¼ hours Serves 4

METRIC/IMPERIAL

150 g/5 oz streaky bacon, with rind removed
1 tablespoon oil
450 g/1 lb onions, coarsely chopped
450 g/1 lb potatoes, thinly sliced
1 (397-g/14-oz) can tomatoes
600 ml/1 pint chicken stock
generous pinch ground mace
1 142-ml/5-fl oz) carton soured cream

Chop the bacon into 1 cm/½ inch pieces and fry in the oil until crisp and golden. Drain the bacon and keep it hot. Fry the onions for 5 minutes, then add the potatoes, tomatoes, stock, mace and half of the bacon. Bring to the boil and simmer for 1 hour. Liquidize in a blender, return to a saucepan, add about half the soured cream and gently reheat, but do not boil. (Add a little milk or water if the soup is too thick.) Serve in individual bowls with a spoonful of the remaining cream and a sprinkling of bacon pieces as garnish.

BORTSCH (Beetroot Soup)

Cooking time 1–1¼ hours Serves 4

METRIC/IMPERIAL

2 onions, finely chopped
1 tablespoon oil
3 beetroots, peeled
175 g/6 oz cabbage, finely sliced
750 ml/1¼ pints beef stock
2 tablespoons vinegar
¼ teaspoon salt and pepper
1 (142-ml/5-fl oz) carton soured cream
chopped parsley to garnish

Fry the onions gently in the oil for about 7 minutes. Chop the beetroots roughly and add to the onions, as well as the cabbage, stock, vinegar and seasoning. Bring to the boil and simmer for about 1 hour in a covered pan. Liquidize in a blender and return to a saucepan to reheat, adding extra liquid if it is too thick. Serve with a spoonful of soured cream and a sprinkling of chopped parsley.

CREAM OF LEEK AND RICE SOUP

Cooking time 15 minutes Serves 4

METRIC/IMPERIAL

25 g/1 oz butter
3–4 leeks, cut into slices
1 teaspoon curry powder
40 g/1½ oz long-grain rice
1 litre/1¾ pints chicken or vegetable stock
150 ml/¼ pint creamy milk
seasoning

To thicken
1 egg yolk
2–3 tablespoons cream or top of milk

Melt the butter in a pressure cooker, add the leeks, cover and sauté, without browning, over a low heat. Draw aside, add the curry powder and cook for 1–2 minutes. Add the rice and stock and bring to the boil. Pressure cook at 15 lb for 12 minutes. Allow the pan to cool at room temperature for about 30 minutes. Add the milk to the soup and liquidize in a blender, or sieve. Rinse out the pan, return the soup to it, reheat and season to taste, adding the egg yolk and cream, mixed together. Do not allow the soup to boil.

FISH SOUP

Cooking time 35–40 minutes Serves 4

METRIC/IMPERIAL

450 g/1 lb any white fish
1.15 litres/2 pints chicken stock
150 ml/¼ pint olive oil
3 large onions, finely chopped
½ clove garlic, crushed
75 g/3 oz tomato purée
1 kg/2 lb tomatoes, peeled and chopped
1 bay leaf
1 teaspoon paprika
seasoning
chopped parsley to garnish

Cook the fish gently in a little of the stock until it begins to flake, about 10 minutes. Remove all the skin and bones and flake the flesh further. Heat the oil in a large saucepan and gently fry the onions and garlic until soft, add the tomato purée, stock (plus that in which the fish was cooked), chopped tomatoes, bay leaf, paprika and seasoning. Simmer for 20 minutes. Add the flaked fish and reheat. Serve garnished with parsley.

SEAFOOD BISQUE

Cooking time 10 minutes Serves 6

METRIC/IMPERIAL

3 tablespoons flour
1 teaspoon mild curry powder
3 tablespoons butter
900 ml/1½ pints milk
4 tablespoons finely chopped spring onions
1 small can clams (optional)
3 scallops, cooked
100 g/4 oz prepared prawns
seasoning
150 ml/¼ pint dry white wine
2 tablespoons finely chopped parsley to garnish

Cook the flour and curry powder in the butter for a few minutes, add the milk and bring to the boil, stirring. Add the spring onions and simmer gently for 5 minutes. Cut the clams and scallops into medium pieces and add the prawns and any clam juice from the can. Reheat, seasoning to taste and adding the wine. Garnish with a sprinkling of chopped parsley.

LEEK AND SALMON SOUP

Cooking time 15–20 minutes Serves 4–6

METRIC/IMPERIAL

2 large leeks
1 large onion
1 large carrot
1–2 sticks celery
2 tablespoons oil
1 tablespoon flour
2 tablespoons tomato purée
750 ml/1¼ pints stock
seasoning
2 teaspoons Worcestershire sauce
grated rind and juice of 1 lemon
1 (227-g/8-oz) can pink salmon
chopped parsley to garnish

Prepare all the vegetables and chop them finely. Sauté in hot oil for 3–4 minutes. Cover the saucepan and allow to cook through without browning. Stir in the flour, add all the other ingredients, ending with the lightly flaked salmon. Bring to the boil and simmer gently for 10–15 minutes. Serve garnished with chopped parsley.

GAZPACHO

Serves 8–10
(as this is really a party soup, large quantities are given)

METRIC/IMPERIAL

1 (793-g/1¾-lb) can tomatoes
1 (540-g/19-oz) can tomato juice
2 teaspoons sugar
1 teaspoon chopped parsley
pinch thyme, dried if necessary
3 tablespoons olive oil
2 tablespoons wine vinegar
1 green pepper, diced
2 large sticks celery, diced
10 spring onions, chopped
1 cucumber, diced – no need to peel
600 ml/1 pint chicken stock
1 clove garlic, crushed
salt
black pepper

To garnish
chopped chives
croûtons

Place the tomatoes and tomato juice in a large bowl and add the sugar, parsley, thyme, olive oil and vinegar. Add half the diced and chopped pepper, celery, onions and cucumber to the tomato mixture. Add the chicken stock and garlic. Then liquidize in a blender for a very short time (only seconds) so as not to purée the vegetables. It may be necessary, with this large quantity, to divide the mixture into two or three and blend separately. Season to taste. Serve very well chilled, garnished with chopped chives. The remaining diced vegetables and croûtons are usually served in separate dishes for guests to help themselves.

Main Courses

This section was lovely to write for it combines all my favourite recipes, some familiar, some new to you I hope. Some are inexpensive and quick for the days which happen all too often, when we are short of both time and money. Others fall into the slightly more luxurious class for when we feel more creative and we've something to celebrate. Whichever the category, the common denominator is that they all taste good!

BOUILLABAISSE

Cooking time 35 minutes Serves 6

METRIC/IMPERIAL

3 onions, finely chopped
1 carrot, finely chopped
150 ml/¼ pint salad oil
1.5 kg/3 lb filleted fish (mixture of cod, haddock, whiting, flounder, plaice etc.)
750 ml/1¼ pints fish stock or water
1 bay leaf
1 (227-g/8-oz) can tomatoes
12 oysters or clams (canned will do)
150 g/5 oz prawns, peeled
2 red peppers, seeded and finely chopped
2 teaspoons salt
½ teaspoon paprika
2 tablespoons lemon juice
2 tablespoons chopped parsley to garnish

Fry the onions and carrot in the oil in a large saucepan for 5 minutes. Add the fish, cut into small pieces, cooked for 5 minutes, then add the stock, bay leaf and tomatoes. Cover and simmer gently (do not allow to boil) for about 20 minutes, until the fish is tender. Add all the other ingredients and heat thoroughly. Serve garnished with chopped parsley.

FISH PLAKI

Cooking time 40 minutes Serves 4

METRIC/IMPERIAL

seasoning
1 tablespoon lemon juice
4 cod (or haddock) steaks
2 large onions, sliced
1 clove garlic, crushed
150 ml/¼ pint cooking oil
3 tomatoes, peeled and quartered
4 tablespoons Worcestershire sauce
2 tablespoons chopped parsley
150 ml/¼ pint water
½ lemon, sliced

Sprinkle salt, pepper and the lemon juice on to the fish. Fry the onions and garlic in the oil until gently browned. Add the tomatoes, Worcestershire sauce, parsley and water and bring to the boil, then cook for 5 minutes. Add the fish to the pan with a slice of lemon on each steak, cover the pan and poach for about 30 minutes. Serve the fish on the bed of vegetables, either hot or cold.

INDIAN SOLE KNOTS

Cooking time 15 minutes Serves 4

METRIC/IMPERIAL

2 dessert apples
4 tomatoes
150 ml/¼ pint milk
150 ml/¼ pint cream
4 fillets of sole
1 large onion, chopped
50 g/2 oz butter
1 tablespoon curry powder
seasoning

To garnish
lemon wedges
chopped parsley

Peel, core and chop the apples. Peel, seed and chop the tomatoes. Add the milk to the cream. Skin each fillet and cut into 4 long thin strips, then tie each strip into a single knot. Fry the onion in the butter until transparent. Add the curry powder and fry for 1 minute. Add the apples and tomatoes and fry for 5 minutes. Add the cream mixture and bring gently to the boil. Season. Add the sole knots and simmer for 8–10 minutes. Serve with boiled rice and garnish with lemon wedges and chopped parsley.

Variation
Large fillets of plaice may be used instead of sole.

SEAFOOD CASSEROLE

Cooking time 30 minutes Serves 6
Oven temperature Moderate 180°C, 350°F, Gas Mark 4

METRIC/IMPERIAL

225 g/8 oz shell pasta
15 g/½ oz butter
1 tablespoon lemon juice
1 teaspoon celery salt
1 teaspoon soy sauce
large bunch spring onions
1 (500-g/15-oz) can lobster soup
450 g/1 lb white crab meat
150 g/5 oz prawns
50 g/2 oz Cheddar cheese, grated

Barely cook (about 8 minutes) the pasta in plenty of boiling salted water. Drain the pasta and place in a buttered ovenproof dish. Add the lemon juice, celery salt, soy sauce and spring onions to the soup and heat through. Stir the flaked crab meat and prawns carefully into the soup mixture. Pour over the pasta and cover with the grated cheese. Bake, uncovered, in a moderate oven until bubbly brown on top.

Variation
Any combination of shellfish may be used: crab, lobster, crawfish, prawns, shrimps, scallops.

KIPPER STAR PIE

Cooking time 35 minutes Serves 8
Oven temperature Hot 220°C, 425°F, Gas Mark 7

METRIC/IMPERIAL

2 (250-g/7½-oz) packets frozen shortcrust pastry, thawed
8 kippers, on the bone
8 spring onions, chopped
2 tomatoes, peeled
1 lemon
1 tablespoon chopped parsley
1 egg, beaten

Roll out each packet of pastry thinly into the largest possible circle. Skin and bone the kippers, keeping the tails intact. Place 1 chopped spring onion and one quarter tomato, sliced, on each kipper and fold over in half. Squeeze the lemon juice and sprinkle a little parsley on each kipper. Place the kippers in star fashion on one circle of pastry, with the tails extending slightly over the edges of the circle. Brush with beaten egg between kippers. Cover with the second piece of pastry, sealing the edges well. Brush the top with egg and bake in a hot oven. Serve hot or cold.

ONION PUDDING

Cooking time 3 hours Serves 3–4
Oven temperature Moderate 160°C, 325°F, Gas Mark 3

METRIC/IMPERIAL

Filling
4 large onions, chopped
2 tablespoons breadcrumbs
¼ teaspoon sage
seasoning
50 g/2 oz butter

Pastry
100 g/4 oz butter
225 g/8 oz plain flour
50 g/2 oz fresh breadcrumbs
1 teaspoon baking powder
generous pinch salt

Bake all the filling ingredients in a covered dish for approximately 1 hour. Rub the butter into the flour and breadcrumbs, add the baking powder and salt and enough water to form a fairly stiff paste. Roll out the pastry and line a basin, fill with the cooled filling and cover with a pastry lid. Cover the basin top with two or three folds of greased paper and steam for 2 hours. Serve with a good brown sauce.

MEDITERRANEAN BAKE

Cooking time 50–55 minutes Serves 4–6
Oven temperature Moderately hot 190°C, 375°F, Gas Mark 5

METRIC/IMPERIAL

450 g/1 lb aubergines, thinly sliced
1 tablespoon salt
1 tablespoon oil
450 g/1 lb onions, chopped
1 (397-g/14-oz) can tomatoes
1 teaspoon basil
2 teaspoons oregano
seasoning
100 g/4 oz fresh breadcrumbs
100 g/4 oz cheese, grated
150 g/6 oz ham, cooked and sliced

Put the aubergines in a saucepan with the salt. Cover with boiling water and boil gently for 2 minutes, then drain. Heat the oil in a frying pan, add the onions and cook over a low heat until softened. Add the tomatoes, herbs and seasoning and cook for about 10 minutes until the sauce is reduced by about one-third. Season to taste. Mix the breadcrumbs and cheese together. Lightly oil a 1.5 litre/2½ pint ovenproof dish. Make layers of the igredients: first put half the aubergines in the base of the dish, cover with half the tomato sauce, then a third of the crumb mixture, followed by half the ham. Repeat the layers, finishing with the remaining third of the crumb mixture. Cover with a lid or foil. Bake in a moderate oven for 40 minutes, uncovering the dish for the last 5 minutes to brown the top. Serve warm, or cold with a green salad.

RAGOÛT OF BEEF

Cooking time 1½ hours Serves 2–3

METRIC/IMPERIAL

500 g/18 oz chuck steak, cubed
2 tablespoons seasoned flour
2 tablespoons oil
8 small onions, peeled
300 ml/½ pint beef stock
150 ml/¼ pint claret
25 g/1 oz butter
6 tablespoons chopped celery
4 tablespoons chopped walnuts
rind of 1 orange, cut into thin strips and blanched for 4 minutes

Toss the steak in the seasoned flour and fry in the oil until it is browned on all sides. Add the onions and any remaining flour, stirring well. Add the stock and claret, bring to the boil and then simmer gently in a covered pan until the meat is tender. Meanwhile, sauté the celery, walnuts and blanched orange rind in the butter. Serve the ragoût with the celery/nut mixture scattered on top.

BEEF IN RED WINE

Cooking time 2¼ hours Serves 4

METRIC/IMPERIAL

800 g/1¾ lb topside beef, cut into cubes
¼ bottle Burgundy
4–6 tablespoons oil
50 g/2 oz seasoned flour
600 ml/1 pint beef stock
75 g/3 oz bacon pieces, chopped
2 large onions, sliced
2 carrots, sliced
25 g/1 oz tomato purée
generous pinch thyme and marjoram
1 bay leaf
1 clove garlic, crushed
225 g/8 oz small mushrooms
chopped parsley to garnish

Marinate the meat overnight in the wine plus 2 tablespoons of the oil in a covered container in the refrigerator. Drain the beef well, toss in seasoned flour and fry quickly in hot oil until browned on all sides. Add the stock and bring up to simmering. Fry the bacon, adding the onions, carrots, tomato purée, herbs, bay leaf and garlic and cook for 2–3 minutes. Add the vegetables to the stock and beef, together with the wine marinade and mushrooms. Simmer gently for 2 hours, until the meat is tender. Remove the bay leaf, check seasoning to taste and serve garnished with the chopped parsley.

GOULASH

Cooking time 2–2½ hours Serves 4
Oven temperature Moderate 160°C, 325°F, Gas Mark 3

METRIC/IMPERIAL

675 g/1½ lb stewing steak, cubed
20 g/¾ oz seasoned flour
50 g/2 oz margarine
2 large onions, chopped
1 green pepper, seeded and chopped
2 teaspoons paprika
150 ml/¼ pint tomato juice
1 tablespoon tomato purée
300 ml/½ pint beef stock
seasoning

Toss the meat in the seasoned flour to coat, and sauté in the margarine for 10–15 minutes until well browned. Add the onions, green pepper and paprika, stir well and cook for a further 5 minutes, then add the tomato juice, purée, beef stock and seasoning to taste. Place the contents in an ovenproof, lidded casserole and cook for 1½–2 hours until the meat is tender. Serve with pasta or rice.

WORCESTER COUNTRY CASSEROLE

Cooking time 3 hours 15 minutes Serves 6
Oven temperature Moderate 160°C, 325°F, Gas Mark 3

METRIC/IMPERIAL

Marinade
4 tablespoons Worcestershire sauce
4 tablespoons water
1 teaspoon salt

Casserole
575 g/1¼ lb steak and kidney
25 g/1 oz dripping
2 onions, chopped
3 sticks celery, chopped
2 medium parsnips, chopped
3 medium carrots, sliced
25 g/1 oz flour
300 ml/½ pint water
450 g/1 lb tomatoes, peeled and chopped
¼ teaspoon mixed dried herbs
100 g/4 oz mushrooms, sliced

Mix together the Worcestershire sauce, water and salt for the marinade. Place the steak and kidney in a shallow dish and pour over the marinade. Leave to marinate in a refrigerator for 4 hours, or overnight, turning occasionally. Drain the meat and reserve the marinade.

Heat the dripping in a large frying pan and brown the meat on all sides. Remove the meat from the pan with a draining spoon and place in a casserole. Add the onions, celery, parsnips and carrots to the pan and cook gently for 10 minutes. Stir in the flour and cook for 1–2 minutes. Remove from the heat and gradually stir in the water. Return to the heat and bring to the boil, stirring all the time. Add the tomatoes, reserved marinade and herbs. Pour over the meat in the casserole, stir, cover and cook in a moderate oven for 3 hours. Add the mushrooms 30 minutes before the end of cooking.

BOEUF STROGONOFF

Cooking Time 10–15 minutes Serves 4

METRIC/IMPERIAL

4 rump steaks
100 g/4 oz butter
1 onion, finely chopped
225 g/8 oz button mushrooms, thinly sliced
seasoning
1 tablespoon lemon juice
300 ml/½ pint single cream

Cut each rump steak into 1 cm/½ inch strips. Melt half the butter in a heavy-based frying pan and fry the onion until transparent. Add the strips of steak and fry for about 5 minutes, until tender. Remove the steak, add the rest of the butter and cook the mushrooms. Replace the steak and season to taste. Stir the lemon juice into the cream and pour into the pan and heat through carefully.

Serve with a border of boiled rice, garnished with a little chopped parsley.

CARBONNADE OF BEEF

Cooking time 2 hours Serves 6
Oven temperature Moderate 160°C, 325°F, Gas Mark 3

METRIC/IMPERIAL

1.5 kg/3 lb stewing steak, cubed
75 g/3 oz butter or margarine
3 onions, sliced
2 cloves garlic, crushed
100 g/4 oz bacon, chopped
50 g/2 oz flour
450 ml/¾ pint beer
450 ml/¾ pint beef stock
½ teaspoon ground nutmeg
1½ tablespoons vinegar
1 teaspoon sugar
1 bay leaf
seasoning

To garnish
French bread, sliced and spread with French mustard
parsley

Brown the meat in the fat for about 5 minutes. Place in an ovenproof casserole. Sauté the onions, garlic and bacon, then stir in the flour and brown slightly. Gradually add the beer and stock, plus the nutmeg, vinegar, sugar, bay leaf and seasoning. Bring to the boil and pour over the meat in the casserole. Cover and bake for 1½ hours. Remove the casserole lid and place slices of French bread, mustard side uppermost, on top of the meat. Return to the oven for 30 minutes, until crisp. Garnish with parsley.

BRAISED BEEF WITH CHESTNUTS

Cooking time 2 hours Serves 4–6
Oven temperature Moderate 160°C, 325°F, Gas Mark 3

METRIC/IMPERIAL

675 g/1½ lb chuck steak, cut into 3.5-cm/1½-inch cubes
225 g/8 oz belly pork, cut into 1-cm/½-inch cubes
50 g/2 oz lard
2 large onions, chopped
2 sticks celery, chopped
50 g/2 oz flour
600 ml/1 pint beef stock
225 g/8 oz chestnuts
3 tablespoons Worcestershire sauce
seasoning
1 tablespoon port

Fry the beef and pork in the fat for about 8 minutes until browned, stirring frequently. Remove the meat and place in a 2.25-litre/4-pint casserole. Fry the onions and celery in the remaining fat for 5 minutes, add the flour, cook for a further 2 minutes, and then blend in the stock. Boil the chestnuts for 10 minutes and skin, then add to the mixture. Bring to the boil, add the Worcestershire sauce and seasoning. Pour over the meat in the casserole and cook in a moderate oven until the meat is tender. Stir in the port before serving.

BEEF BOURGUIGNONNE

Cooking time 1½–2 hours Serves 4
Oven temperature Moderate 160°C, 325°F, Gas Mark 3

METRIC/IMPERIAL

675 g/1½ lb stewing steak, cubed
20 g/¾ oz flour
seasoning
12 small button onions
100 g/4 oz streaky bacon, chopped
25 g/1 oz margarine or butter
300 ml/½ pint beef stock
300 ml/½ pint red wine
½ teaspoon ground nutmeg
pinch thyme and sage
100 g/4 oz small button mushrooms
1 clove garlic, crushed

To garnish
fried triangles of bread
chopped parsley

Toss the meat in the seasoned flour, then sauté with the onions and bacon in the fat for about 10 minutes, until brown. Add any leftover flour and blend in the beef stock and wine. Add all the remaining ingredients, seasoning to taste, place in a lidded casserole and cook in a moderate oven until the meat is tender. Serve with fried bread triangles bordering the dish and garnish with chopped parsley.

SUKI YAKI

Cooking time 20–25 minutes Serves 4

METRIC/IMPERIAL

10 large spring onions
3 tablespoons beef stock
1 teaspoon sugar
1½ tablespoons soy sauce
1 teaspoon Worcestershire sauce
2–3 tablespoons olive oil
450 g/1 lb frying steak, cut into thin strips
1 onion, thinly sliced
225 g/8 oz Chinese cabbage, shredded
100 g/4 oz mushrooms, thinly sliced
450 g/1 lb bamboo shoots or bean sprouts
seasoning

Prepare the spring onions in the normal way, but cut them in half lengthways. Prepare all the other ingredients, so that cooking can be done speedily, which is the essence of this dish. Combine the stock, sugar, soy sauce, and Worcestershire sauce and seasoning in a bowl and blend together well.

Heat the oil, using a large frying pan or wok and first fry the beef strips to brown quickly on all sides and push meat to one side of the pan. Fry the onions until soft, set to another side of the pan and fry the spring onions, then the Chinese cabbage, mushrooms, with the bamboo shoots last, trying to keep all the ingredients as separate as possible. Add the beef stock and boil quickly for 3–4 minutes. Serve with plain boiled rice.

CHINESE PEPPER STEAK

Cooking time 20 minutes Serves 4

METRIC/IMPERIAL

575 g/1¼ lb rump steak
150 ml/¼ pint dry sherry
2½ tablespoons oil
seasoning
3 tablespoons finely chopped spring onions
1 clove garlic, crushed
2 medium green peppers, seeded and chopped
4 sticks celery, sliced
150 ml/¼ pint beef stock and marinade
1½ tablespoons cornflour
2–3 tablespoons water
1 teaspoon soy sauce

Cut the steak into thin strips, across the grain, and marinate in the sherry. Drain, reserving the sherry. Brown the meat in the oil in a large frying pan. Add the seasoning, onions, garlic, peppers and celery and mix together for a minute or two. Add the stock plus sherry, cover the pan tightly and cook over a moderate heat for 7–10 minutes until the meat is tender, but the vegetables are still slightly crisp. Blend the cornflour with the water and soy sauce and add to the pan, stirring continually until the sauce has thickened. Serve immediately with rice or noodles.

SWISS STEAK SPECIAL

Cooking time 1 hour Serves 2
Oven temperature Moderately hot 200°C, 400°F, Gas Mark 6

METRIC/IMPERIAL

100 g/4 oz butter
1 clove garlic, crushed
1 packet onion soup mix (2 servings)
450 g/1 lb rump steak, cut thickly
freshly ground black pepper
3 tablespoons red wine
150 g/5 oz mushrooms, sliced

Spread half of the butter over the centre of a large piece of aluminium foil folded double thickness. Add the crushed garlic and sprinkle half the packet of soup over the butter. Place the steak on top with the black pepper, remaining soup mix and butter. Pour over the wine and cover with the mushrooms. Fold the foil into a parcel, to prevent the juices from running out, and bake for about an hour.

TASTY STEAK

Cooking time 30 minutes Serves 4
Oven temperature Moderately hot 200°C, 400°F, Gas Mark 6

METRIC/IMPERIAL

4 rump or sirloin steaks
25 g/1 oz butter
50 g/2 oz onion, chopped
50 g/2 oz celery, chopped
2 tablespoons brown sugar
1 tablespoon mustard
2 teaspoons salt
1 teaspoon paprika
1 tablespoon tomato purée
2 tablespoons Worcestershire sauce
2 tablespoons vinegar
2 tablespoons lemon juice
150 ml/¼ pint water

Brown the steaks in the butter in a frying pan. Remove to a 1.5 litre/ 2½ pint ovenproof dish. Gently fry the onion and celery in the remaining butter until the onion is pale golden. Add all the dry ingredients to the pan and then all the liquid ones. Pour the sauce mixture over the steaks and cover with a lid or foil. Bake in a moderately hot oven until the steak is quite tender. Serve the steak in its sauce with boiled rice.

Variation
Tougher cuts of steak may be used, with correspondingly longer cooking time.

SPICY MEAT KEBABS

Cooking time 10 minutes Serves 4

METRIC/IMPERIAL

Marinade

4 tablespoooons wine
2 teaspoons Worcestershire sauce
½ teaspoon chilli powder
½ teaspoon allspice
seasoning

225 g/8 oz best grilling steak
100 g/4 oz streaky bacon
8 pickled onions
8 button mushrooms
1 large tomato, cut into 8 pieces
1 pig's kidney, cored and cut into 8 pieces
4 frankfurter sausages, cut in half
25 g/1 oz margarine or butter, melted
chopped parsley to garnish

Combine all the marinade ingredients. Cut the meat into medium pieces and place in the marinade mixture for 2–3 hours. Roll up the bacon slices tightly. Skewer all the ingredients on to 4 long (or 8 short) skewers. Add the melted butter to the marinade remaining when the meat is threaded on to the skewers and use this to baste the skewers continually during cooking. Preheat the grill and cook for about 10 minutes. Serve with rice and garnish with the chopped parsley.

AUSTRALIAN MEAT AND POTATO PIE

Cooking time 1 hour 10 minutes Serves 4
Oven temperature Moderate 180°C, 350°F, Gas Mark 4

METRIC/IMPERIAL

500 g/18 oz raw minced beef
2 onions, finely chopped
seasoning
1 (298-g/10½-oz) can tomato soup
½ green pepper, seeded and chopped
1 kg/2 lb potatoes, peeled and boiled
50 g/2 oz butter
4 tablespoons milk
6 tablespoons grated cheese
1 tablespoon chopped parsley

Fry the minced beef with three-quarters of the onion and seasoning, until the meat begins to brown. Add the soup and simmer, covered, for 20–25 minutes. Add the chopped pepper, mix well and place in a deep ovenproof dish.

Mash the cooked potatoes, adding half the butter and the milk; beat well. Add the remaining onion, grated cheese, parsley and seasoning. Place on top of the meat mixture and dot the top with the remaining butter. Bake until the topping is browned, about 45 minutes.

MOUSSAKA 1

Cooking time 50 minutes–1 hour Serves 4
Oven temperature Moderate 180°C, 350°F, Gas Mark 4

METRIC/IMPERIAL

3 aubergines, sliced
little flour
300 ml/½ pint oil
4 onions, thinly sliced
450 g/1 lb minced beef
4 tomatoes, peeled and sliced
seasoning
150 ml/¼ pint thick tomato pulp, or 2 tablespoons tomato purée
150 ml/¼ pint beef stock
2 large eggs
150 ml/¼ pint single cream
50 g/2 oz cheese, grated

Dust the aubergine slices with flour and fry in the oil until lightly browned, remove from the frying pan and sauté the onions, then the minced beef. Layer the aubergines, onions, tomatoes and beef in an ovenproof dish, seasoning each layer. Mix together the tomato purée and stock and pour over. Bake uncovered for 30–40 minutes in a moderate oven. Beat together the eggs and cream, pour over the casserole, sprinkle with the grated cheese and bake for a further 20 minutes, until firm and golden.

MOUSSAKA 2

Cooking time 1 hour 30 minutes Serves 4
Oven temperature Cool 150°C, 300°F, Gas Mark 2 – 1 hour
Moderate 180°C, 350°F, Gas Mark 4 – 20 minutes

METRIC/IMPERIAL

3 medium aubergines
300 ml/½ pint oil
350 g/12 oz onions, finely chopped
450–575 g/1–1¼ lb minced beef or lamb
pinch cinnamon
3 tablespoons chopped parsley
½ teaspoon sugar
1 clove garlic, crushed
seasoning
2 teaspoons tomato purée
200 ml/7 fl oz beef stock
4 tablespoons grated cheese
300 ml/½ pint Béchamel sauce (see page 174)

Cut the aubergines into slices (about 5 mm/¼ inches) and put aside with a liberal sprinkling of salt for an hour. Rinse them and dab dry with kitchen paper, before frying gently in the oil until soft. Remove and keep warm. Fry the onions until they are beginning to brown, then add the meat, cinnamon, parsley, sugar and garlic and cook until the meat has browned. Layer the aubergines and meat mixture alternately in a greased ovenproof dish, seasoning each layer. Begin and end with the aubergines. Heat through the tomato purée and stock, pour this over the dish and bake slowly for about 1 hour.

Add 3 tablespoons of the grated cheese to the Béchamel sauce and pour over the dish, sprinkling the top with the remaining grated cheese. Brown in a moderate oven for about 20 minutes.

CHILLI CON CARNE

Cooking time 45–60 minutes Serves 6

METRIC/IMPERIAL

2 onions, chopped
1 green pepper, chopped
3 sticks celery, chopped
1 clove garlic, crushed
175 g/6 oz carrots, chopped
50 g/2 oz butter or margarine
675 g/1½ lb raw minced beef
1 (227-g/8-oz) can tomatoes
10 prunes, soaked overnight and stoned
450 ml/¾ pint beef stock
1 teaspoon Worcestershire sauce
1 tablespoon chilli powder
1½ tablespoons tomato purée
salt
black pepper
1 (297-g/14-oz) can red kidney beans, drained and rinsed
chopped parsley to garnish

Sauté the onions, green pepper, celery, garlic and carrots in the butter for about 10 minutes. Add the meat and fry for a further 5 minutes before adding all the other ingredients, except the beans and parsley. Cover and cook over a gentle heat for about 40–45 minutes. Stir occasionally and add a little water, if it appears too dry. When the meat and vegetables are tender, add the beans, bring the mixture to the boil and simmer for a few minutes. Garnish with chopped parsley.

NORTH COUNTRY POTATO HOT-POT

Cooking time 1½ hours Serves 4
Oven temperature Moderate 180°C, 350°F, Gas Mark 4

METRIC/IMPERIAL

1 tablespoon oil
100 g/4 oz streaky bacon, chopped
1 large onion, chopped
450 g/1 lb raw minced beef
1 (227-g/8-oz) can tomatoes
2 tablespoons Worcestershire sauce
1 tablespoon tomato purée
½ teaspoon basil
150 ml/¼ pint stock
seasoning
1 large onion, sliced
450 g/1 lb potatoes, peeled and sliced
15 g/½ oz butter, melted

Heat the oil in a large pan, add the bacon and chopped onion and fry gently for 5 minutes. Add the minced beef and fry until evenly browned, then add the tomatoes, Worcestershire sauce, tomato purée, basil, stock and seasoning to taste. Bring to the boil, reduce the heat and simmer gently for 20 minutes. Cook the sliced onion and potato in boiling salted water for 3–4 minutes, until the potato is just cooked and drain well. Spoon half the meat mixture into a 1·5 litre/2½ pint ovenproof dish and cover with half the potatoes and onion. Spoon the remaining meat mixture over the top and overlap the rest of the potatoes and onion to cover completely. Brush with the melted butter and bake in a moderate oven for 1 hour.

HOMESPUN LOAF

Cooking time 1 hour Serves 2–4
Oven temperature Moderate 180°C, 350°F, Gas Mark 4

METRIC/IMPERIAL

225 g/8 oz potatoes
1 large onion
1 cooking apple
450 g/1 lb minced beef
225 g/8 oz sausage meat
1 egg
3 tablespoons milk
2 teaspoons salt
pinch pepper

Peel and grate the potatoes, onion and apple. Mix in all the other ingredients until evenly balanced. Pack into two greased 0.5 kg/1 lb loaf tins and bake in a moderate oven for 1 hour. Leave for 5 minutes to set.

NUTTY 'BURGERS

Cooking time 6 minutes Serves 4

METRIC/IMPERIAL

1 large onion, grated
450 g/1 lb raw minced beef
seasoning
2 teaspoons Worcestershire sauce
25 g/1 oz peanuts, chopped
1 egg, lightly beaten
flour if needed
1 tablespoon oil
25 g/1 oz margarine

Mix the onion, beef, seasoning, Worcestershire sauce and peanuts together with the beaten egg. Divide the mixture into eight equal portions and shape into rounds, about 5 mm/¼ inch thick. Add a little flour if the mixture proves difficult to handle.

Fry the burgers in the oil and margarine mixture for about 3 minutes on each side, until golden brown.

LAMB PAPRIKA

Cooking time 1½–2 hours
Oven temperature Moderate 180°C, 350°F, Gas Mark 4

METRIC/IMPERIAL

675 g/1½ lb boned leg of lamb
25 g/1 oz flour
1 large onion, chopped
1 clove garlic, crushed
25 g/1 oz margarine or butter
1 (198-g/7-oz) can pimientos
1 (227-g/8-oz) can tomatoes
2 tablespoons paprika
pinch brown sugar
1 teaspoon Worcestershire sauce
2 bay leaves
1 teaspoon celery salt
seasoning
1 (150-g/5.3-oz) carton natural yogurt
chopped parsley

Cut the lamb into 2.5 cm/1 inch cubes and toss in the flour. Sauté the onion, garlic and meat in the hot fat for 5 minutes.

Drain and slice the pimientos, add with all the other ingredients, except the yogurt and parsley and place in a lidded ovenproof casserole. Cook in a moderate oven for 1½–2 hours, until the meat is tender. Just before serving pour over the yogurt and sprinkle with chopped parsley.

LAMB CHOPS IN PARCELS

Cooking time 45 minutes Serves 4
Oven temperature Moderately hot 200°C, 400°F, Gas Mark 6

METRIC/IMPERIAL

4 thick lamb chops
4 slices lamb's liver
4 small onions, chopped
1 clove garlic, crushed
seasoning
1 tablespoon chopped parsley
1 tablespoon olive oil
2 tablespoons dry white wine

Place the lamb chops on a large piece of aluminium foil. Cover each chop with a slice of liver, chopped onion, garlic, salt, pepper and parsley. Divide the oil and wine between each chop. Fold up the foil into a loose parcel. Bake in a moderately hot oven for 45 minutes.

Serve with jacket potatoes (with chive butter), cooked at the same time.

DEVON PIE

Cooking time 1½ hours Serves 4
Oven temperature Moderately hot 190°C, 375°F, Gas Mark 5 – 15 minutes Cool 150°C, 300°F, Gas Mark 2 – 1¼ hours

METRIC/IMPERIAL

8 best end of neck lamb cutlets, trimmed
6 leeks, peeled and thinly sliced
4 apples, peeled, cored and sliced
generous pinch nutmeg and allspice
2 tablespoons sugar
seasoning
600 ml/1 pint dry cider
368-g/13-oz packet frozen shortcrust pastry – thawed
little milk

Using a 1.5 litre (3 pint pie dish) put half the chops in the bottom of the dish. Cover with a layer of leeks, apples, spices, sugar and seasonings. Add the cider, then the remaining chops. Roll out the pastry and cover the pie. Brush with a little milk and bake first at the higher temperature for 15 minutes, then cover the pie with foil, reduce the oven temperature and cook for a further 1¼ hours.

BAMI

Cooking time 20 minutes Serves 6

METRIC/IMPERIAL

- 500 g/18 oz fillet of pork, cut into 2.5-cm/1-inch pieces
- ½ small white cabbage, finely shredded
- ½ small head celery, finely shredded
- 1 onion, finely chopped
- 1 clove garlic, crushed
- 2 tablespoons oil
- 100 g/4 oz cooked prawns
- generous pinch powdered ginger
- 2 tablespoons dry sherry
- seasoning
- 250 g/9 oz egg noodles, cooked
- 2 eggs
- 1 tablespoon milk
- 1 teaspoon chopped chives

Blanch the pork pieces in boiling water for 5 minutes. Remove the pork, add the cabbage and celery to this water and boil quickly with the lid on the pan for 3–4 minutes. Fry the onion, garlic and meat in the oil and brown slightly. Add the well-drained cabbage and celery and the prawns, ginger and sherry. Stir well to combine the flavours, adjust seasoning to taste and then stir in the cooked egg noodles. Cover and keep hot. Beat the eggs and milk together with salt and pepper. Pour into a large greased frying pan, to make a thin omelette. Turn out flat on to a board and cut into thin strips for garnish. Pile the meat and noodle mixture on to a warmed oval dish and arrange the egg strips, lattice-fashion, on top. Sprinkle with the chives and serve very hot.

PORK AND APPLE CASSEROLE

Cooking time 1 hour 10 minutes Serves 4
Oven temperature Moderate 180°C, 350°F, Gas Mark 4

METRIC/IMPERIAL

- 1 large onion, sliced into rings
- 2 tablespoons oil
- 575 g/1¼ lb pork leg fillet
- 25 g/1 oz flour
- 300 ml/½ pint dry cider
- 150 ml/¼ pint chicken stock
- ½ teaspoon cinnamon
- 1 bay leaf
- 2 red-skinned apples
- 1 (142-ml/5-fl oz) carton soured cream
- seasoning

Fry the onion rings in oil for 2–3 minutes. Trim any fat from the pork, cut into 2.5 cm/1 inch pieces, add to the onions and fry to seal in the juices, tossing frequently. Stir in the flour and cook for about one minute. Gradually add the cider and stock, stirring all the time and bring to the boil, then add the cinnamon and bay leaf. Transfer to an ovenproof casserole and bake for about an hour until the meat is tender. Core and quarter the apples (do not peel) and add to the casserole 10 minutes before the end of the cooking time. Stir in the soured cream before serving and adjust seasoning to taste.

THATCHED PORK CASSEROLE

Cooking time 1 hour 40–45 minutes Serves 4
Oven temperature Moderate 180°C, 350°F, Gas Mark 4

METRIC/IMPERIAL

575 g/1¼ lb sparerib pork, cut into 2.5-cm/1-inch cubes
25 g/1 oz flour
2 onions, sliced
25 g/1 oz lard
2 cooking apples, peeled, cored and sliced
300 ml/½ pint cider
¼ teaspoon sage
seasoning
6 large slices white bread, 5 mm/¼ inch thick
50 g/2 oz butter, melted

Toss the pork in the flour. Fry the onions in the fat for about 3 minutes. Add the pork and brown on all sides. Stir in any remaining flour. Add the apples, cider, sage and seasoning and bring to the boil, stirring. Transfer to a 2.25 litre/4 pint ovenproof casserole and cook covered for 1 hour. Remove the crusts from the bread. Cut each slice into 4 strips and arrange overlapping, radiating from the centre. Brush with the melted butter and return to the oven uncovered for 30 minutes, until the bread is crisp and golden.

JAMBALAYA

Cooking time 40–45 minutes Serves 4

METRIC/IMPERIAL

225 g/8 oz onions, sliced
575 g/1¼ lb boneless lean pork, cut into cubes
50 g/2 oz lard
175 g/6 oz long-grain rice
2 tablespoons Worcestershire sauce
½ teaspoon curry powder
225 g/8 oz frozen mixed vegetables, cooked
seasoning

To garnish
2 hard-boiled eggs, sliced
chopped chives

Fry the onions and pork in the fat quickly for 5 minutes. Reduce the heat, cover the pan and simmer for about 30 minutes, stirring frequently. Use a large pan to make room for the later additions to the recipe.

Cook the rice in a large quantity of boiling salted water for 10 minutes. Drain the rice, rinse under the cold tap and drain well again.

When the meat is cooked, stir in the Worcestershire sauce, curry powder, rice, cooked vegetables and seasoning. Reheat the whole dish for about 5 minutes. Serve garnished with slices of hard-boiled eggs and chopped chives.

PORK AND APPLE PIE

Cooking time 1 hour 15–20 minutes Serves 4
Oven temperature Moderately hot 200°C, 400°F, Gas Mark 6

METRIC/IMPERIAL

25 g/1 oz lard
2 large onions, chopped
3 sticks celery, chopped
675 g/1½ lb pork spare-rib or shoulder chops, cut into 2.5-cm/1-inch cubes
2 tablespoons Worcestershire sauce
300 ml/½ pint chicken stock
1 tablespoon cornflour
2 tablespoons water
seasoning
1 large cooking apple, peeled, cored and chopped
175 g/6 oz shortcrust pastry (see page 156)
beaten egg for glazing

Heat the lard in a pan and fry the onions and celery gently for 5 minutes. Add the pork and fry, turning occasionally, for a further 10 minutes. Add the Worcestershire sauce and stock, cover and simmer for 30 minutes. Blend the cornflour with the water and stir into the saucepan. Bring back to the boil, season, add the apple and leave to cool. Place in a 1 litre/1½ pint pie dish.

Roll out the pastry and use to cover the pie dish. Brush with the beaten egg. Bake in a moderately hot oven for 30–35 minutes, until the pastry is golden.

HONEY BAKED PORK CHOPS

Cooking time 1 hour Serves 4
Oven temperature Moderate 180°C, 350°F, Gas Mark 4

METRIC/IMPERIAL

1 onion stock cube
25 g/1 oz flour
4 lean pork chops, trimmed
1 large onion, chopped
40 g/1½ oz margarine
1 tablespoon honey
200 ml/7 fl oz chicken stock
pinch nutmeg
juice of 1 orange
seasoning
100 g/4 oz button mushrooms

To garnish
1 orange, sliced
watercress sprigs

Crumble the onion cube into the flour and toss the chops in this mixture. Fry the chops with the onion in the margarine for about 5 minutes, until browned on both sides. Place the chops and onions in an ovenproof casserole, add any remaining flour to the margarine and cook for 1 minute. Add all the other ingredients except the mushrooms, and bring to the boil, stirring all the time. Pour over the chops and bake for about 40 minutes, add the mushrooms and cook for a further 5 minutes.

Serve each chop garnished with a slice of orange and a watercress.

PORK WITH LEEKS

Cooking time 1¼ hours Serves 2

METRIC/IMPERIAL

350 g/12 oz lean shoulder pork
2 tablespoons vegetable oil
100 g/4 oz leeks
1 tablespoon plain flour
150 ml/¼ pint dry cider
150 ml/¼ pint stock
1 orange
seasoning
450 g/1 lb potatoes
15 g/½ oz butter
little milk

Slice the pork into 2.5 cm/1 inch cubes and brown in the hot oil, then remove from the pan. Slice the prepared leeks thinly and fry to golden brown in the oil. Stir in the flour, add the cider, stock and finely grated orange rind. Season and bring to the boil. Replace the meat, cover and simmer gently for about 1¼ hours or until the pork is tender. Adjust seasoning. Boil the potatoes, mash with the butter and a little milk and season. Remove the pith from the orange and slice thinly. Spoon the meat into a shallow ovenproof dish and pipe the potato on top, leaving a space in the centre. Brown under the grill. Place the orange slices down the centre.

LEEKS IN CIDER

Cooking time 1 hour 10 minutes Serves 4
Oven temperature Moderate 180°C, 350°F, Gas Mark 4

METRIC/IMPERIAL

4 large leeks, cut into 1-cm/½-inch slices
75 g/3 oz butter
300 ml/½ pint dry cider
pinch sage
seasoning
3 dessert apples, cored and sliced
4 rashers belly pork

Sauté the leek slices in the butter until they are beginning to brown. Put in an ovenproof casserole with the cider, sage and seasoning. Cover and cook for approximately 40 minutes. Remove from the oven and layer the unpeeled apple slices over the leeks, laying the pork rashers on top. Return to the oven uncovered, until the pork rashers have browned and are crispy, about 30 minutes.

ECONOMY CASSOULET

Cooking time 1 hour Serves 4
Oven temperature Moderate 180°C, 350°F, Gas Mark 4

METRIC/IMPERIAL

450 g/1 lb haricot beans
225 g/8 oz streaky belly pork
1 large onion, sliced
2 tablespoons black treacle
½ teaspoon Worcestershire sauce
2 teaspoons brown sugar
2 teaspoons dry mustard
seasoning

Soak the beans overnight, then cook them for 1½–2 hours in the water in which they were soaked. Strain the beans and keep the water. Cut the pork into medium pieces. Reheat the bean water, adding the treacle, Worcestershire sauce, brown sugar, mustard and seasoning. Place the beans, pork and onions in a casserole dish, add the 'bean water' sauce and cover with a lid or foil and cook in a moderate oven for about an hour until the beans are soft but not mushy. Add more water if necessary.

BACON PROVENÇAL

Cooking time 1 hour 35–45 minutes Serves 5–6
Oven temperature Moderately hot 200°C, 400°F, Gas Mark 6

METRIC/IMPERIAL

1.25 kg/2½ lb collar bacon joint, boned and rolled
2 cloves garlic, crushed
1 onion stock cube, crumbled
2 tablespoons breadcrumbs
225 g/8 oz button onions, peeled
25 g/1 oz butter or margarine
4 large tomatoes, peeled and quartered
1½ teaspoons oregano
150 ml/¼ pint white wine
seasoning
chopped parsley

Place the bacon in a saucepan covered with water, bring to the boil and then discard the water. Cover with fresh water, bring to the boil and simmer for 1 hour. Remove the joint and strip away the rind. Place the joint in a small roasting tin and cover the fat top of the joint with a mixture of the crushed garlic, crumbled onion cube and breadcrumbs. Sauté the small onions in the butter until they start to brown, add all the other ingredients and bring to the boil, then pour around the bacon joint. Complete cooking, uncovered, for 30–45 minutes until the meat is tender and the topping is crisp.

BURNING LOVE

Cooking time few minutes Serves 4

METRIC/IMPERIAL

675 g/1½ lb potatoes, boiled
little milk, butter, and seasoning
225 g/8 oz streaky bacon, cut into small pieces
2 large onions, sliced
2 tomatoes, peeled, halved and grilled

Mash the cooked potatoes with a little milk, butter and seasoning to taste; keep warm. Fry the bacon pieces until crisp; keep hot. Fry the onions in the bacon fat until soft and tender. To serve, pile the potatoes on to a serving plate, top with the onions and bacon and pour over any bacon fat for extra flavour. Garnish with the tomatoes.

COTTAGE CHEESE AND BACON PUDDING

Cooking time 50–55 minutes Serves 4–6
Oven temperature Hot 220°C, 425°F, Gas Mark 7

METRIC/IMPERIAL

1 onion, chopped
150 g/5 oz streaky bacon, chopped
15 g/½ oz butter
2 tablespoons chopped parsley
50 g/2 oz fresh white breadcrumbs
350 g/12 oz cottage cheese
2 eggs, separated
300 ml/½ pint milk
salt
freshly ground black pepper

Fry the onion and bacon together gently in the butter for 3–4 minutes. Place in a basin and mix with the parsley, breadcrumbs and cottage cheese. Beat the egg yolks into the milk with the seasoning, stir into the cheese mixture and allow to stand for 15 minutes. Whisk the egg whites until they are stiff and fold into the mixture. Turn into a 900 ml/1½ pint ovenproof dish and bake for 35–40 minutes until the pudding is risen and browned. Serve immediately.

LEEK AND BACON PIE

Cooking time 1¼ hours Serves 4–6
Oven temperature Moderate 180°C, 350°F, Gas Mark 4

METRIC/IMPERIAL

Filling

450 g/1 lb bacon joint, boned
50 g/2 oz margarine or butter
450 g/1 lb leeks, sliced
2 green peppers, seeded and thinly sliced
20 g/¾ oz flour
1 onion stock cube, dissolved in 150 ml/¼ pint water
200 ml/7 fl oz double cream
2 egg yolks
pepper
225 g/8 oz cheese pastry (see page 156)
beaten egg for glaze
little Parmesan cheese

Place the bacon joint in the water, bring to the boil and then discard the water. Remove the bacon, cut it into medium cubes and sauté in the fat for 10 minutes. Add the leeks and peppers and cook for a further 5–7 minutes, or until soft. Sprinkle in the flour and stir in well before adding the onion stock, cream, lightly beaten egg yolks and pepper to taste. Allow to cool whilst lining a 20 cm/8 inch flan ring or dish with two-thirds of the cheese pastry. Fill with the bacon/leek mixture and put on the pastry lid firmly. Bake in a moderate oven for 45 minutes, remove and glaze with beaten egg, then sprinkle with the Parmesan and return to the top of the oven to brown for a further 15 minutes.

LEEK PIE

Cooking time 45–50 minutes Serves 4
Oven temperature Hot 230°C, 450°F, Gas Mark 8

METRIC/IMPERIAL

8 young leeks
225 g/8 oz unsmoked bacon, cut thinly
1 small bay leaf
freshly ground black pepper
stock
2 eggs
4 tablespoons cream
225 g/8 oz flaky pastry

Wash and prepare the leeks, leaving on about 7.5 cm/3 inches green leaves. Cut into 2.5 cm/1 inch pieces, then blanch and drain. Remove the rind from the bacon, cut into small dice and blanch. Put the bacon, leeks, bay leaf and pepper into a saucepan, barely cover with stock and simmer for about 15 minutes, when much of the liquid will have evaporated. Lift out into a pie dish and remove the bay leaf. Beat the eggs, add the cream and stir into the juices in the pan. Adjust seasoning, pour over the leeks and cool. Cover with the pastry and bake in a hot oven for 30–35 minutes. Serve hot or cold.

DANISH PIE

Cooking time 30 minutes Serves 4
Oven temperature Moderate 180°C, 350°F, Gas Mark 4

METRIC/IMPERIAL

2 large onions
600 ml/1 pint milk and onion liquor
25 g/1 oz butter
25 g/1 oz flour
seasoning
175–225 g/6–8 oz bacon, diced and cooked
175–225 g/6–8 oz cold cooked potatoes, sliced
2 hard-boiled eggs
2 tomatoes, peeled
1 tablespoon fresh breadcrumbs
1 tablespoon grated cheese

Skin and chop the onions and simmer in a little water for about 10 minutes until soft, then drain. Add milk to the liquid to make up to 600 ml/1 pint. Melt the butter, add the flour, stir for a minute, gradually add the liquid and make a smooth sauce. Season to taste. Layer the bacon, potato, eggs and tomatoes in an ovenproof dish. Add the onions to the sauce and pour over; mix the breadcrumbs and cheese together and sprinkle over the top. Bake in a moderate oven.

BACON AND CORN CASSEROLE

Cooking time 40 minutes Serves 3–4

METRIC/IMPERIAL

100 g/4 oz pasta shells
250 g/9 oz bacon pieces, chopped
2 onions, chopped
1 clove garlic, crushed
½ green pepper, seeded and chopped
1 (397-g/14-oz) can tomatoes
2 tablespoons tomato purée
1 (326-g/11½-oz) can sweet corn
1 (213-g/7½-oz) can mushrooms in sauce
1 tablespoon Worcestershire sauce
3 tablespoons dry sherry
seasoning
triangles of hot toast to garnish

Cook the pasta as directed in a large quantity of boiling water until just tender; drain well. Fry the bacon and when fat runs add the onions, garlic and pepper and fry for about 5 minutes. Add the whole can of tomatoes and the purée, cover and simmer for 15 minutes. Add the drained corn, mushrooms, Worcestershire sauce, sherry and pasta and seasoning to taste. Simmer for a further 15 minutes. Serve in a warmed serving dish, surrounded by triangles of hot toast.

VEAL CACCIATORA

Cooking time 1¾ hours Serves 4–6

METRIC/IMPERIAL

1 onion, chopped
15 g/½ oz butter
1 clove garlic, crushed
675 g/1½ lb lean pie veal, cut into 3.5-cm/1½-inch cubes
2 green peppers, seeded and chopped
1 red pepper, seeded and chopped
6 tomatoes, peeled and quartered
seasoning
1 (142-ml/5-fl oz) carton soured cream
2 tablespoons chopped parsley

Fry the onion in the butter for about 3 minutes. Add the garlic and pie veal and fry for a further 3 minutes. Blanch the peppers in boiling water for half a minute, then add to the veal with the tomatoes and seasoning. Bring to the boil, cover and simmer gently for 1½ hours until the veal is tender. Stir in the soured cream and garnish with the chopped parsley. Serve with plain boiled rice.

LEEKS WITH LAMB'S TONGUES

Cooking time 1½–2 hours Serves 4
Oven temperature Moderate 160°C, 325°F, Gas Mark 3

METRIC/IMPERIAL

4–6 lamb's tongues
4 carrots, sliced
1 turnip, diced
1 stick celery, sliced
2 young leeks, sliced
25 g/1 oz butter or margarine
1 bay leaf
1 tablespoon chopped parsley
½ teaspoon dried thyme
freshly ground black pepper
450 ml/¾ pint beef stock
chopped parsley to garnish

Soak the tongues in salt water for 2 hours and drain. Cover with cold water, bring to the boil, drain again and dab dry with kitchen paper.

Sauté all the prepared vegetables for 5 minutes in the butter, add the herbs and pepper and place in the base of an ovenproof casserole, placing the tongues on top. Pour over the beef stock. Cover and cook in a moderate oven until the tongues are tender. Sprinkle with chopped parsley before serving.

CASSEROLED OX KIDNEYS

Cooking time 1¾ hours Serves 4
Oven temperature Moderate 160°C, 325°F, Gas Mark 3

METRIC/IMPERIAL

450–575 g/1–1¼ lb ox's kidneys
25 g/1 oz seasoned flour
50 g/2 oz dripping or fat
2 large onions
2 rashers streaky bacon
3 tomatoes
stock
leftover red wine

Remove the core from the kidneys and slice them into thin strips. Toss the kidneys in seasoned flour and fry them in hot fat to seal and brown them slightly. Peel and chop the onions, dice the bacon and peel the tomatoes. Remove the kidneys to an ovenproof casserole and fry the bacon and onions together for a few minutes, adding these to the casserole with the thickly sliced tomatoes. Pour in enough stock and wine to cover and seal tightly with a lid or foil. Cook in a moderate oven until the kidney is tender.

KIDNEY, POTATO AND ONION PIE

Cooking time 1 hour Serves 2
Oven temperature Hot 220°C, 425°F, Gas Mark 7 – 10–15 minutes
Moderate 160°C, 325°F, Gas Mark 3 – 45 minutes

METRIC/IMPERIAL

225 g/8 oz shortcrust pastry (see page 156)
350 g/12 oz potatoes, sliced
225 g/8 oz onion, sliced
175 g/6 oz pig's kidney, sliced
seasoning
beaten egg

Line a pie dish with two-thirds of the pastry. Layer the potatoes, onions, kidney then the onions and potatoes again, so that the kidney is in the centre, seasoning well at the kidney stage. Cover the dish with the remaining pastry and brush with the beaten egg to glaze. Bake in a hot, then moderate oven until golden brown.

KIDNEYS AND BABY ONIONS

Cooking time 25 minutes Serves 3–4

METRIC/IMPERIAL

6 lamb's kidneys
100 g/4 oz butter
100 g/4 oz thin frankfurter
  sausages, cut into chunks
12 small onions, peeled and
  blanched
100 g/4 oz button mushrooms
1 tablespoon flour
1 teaspoon tomato purée
1 tablespoon dry sherry
150 ml/¼ pint beef stock } or any combination of the two
2 tablespoons red wine } available
seasoning

To garnish
croûtons
chopped parsley

Skin and cut the kidneys in half lengthways and remove the core. Sauté the kidneys in the butter quickly, add the frankfurters, onions and mushrooms and cook for 2–3 minutes. Stir in the flour, tomato purée, sherry and stock and wine and bring to the boil. Season to taste, then simmer gently for 20 minutes until the kidneys are tender. Serve surrounded by croûtons of fried bread and sprinkled with chopped parsley.

ONIONS AND KIDNEY DUMPLINGS

Cooking time 45 minutes Serves 4
Oven temperature Hot 220°C, 425°F, Gas Mark 7 – 10 minutes
Moderate 180°C, 350° F, Gas Mark 4 – 35 minutes

METRIC/IMPERIAL

8 medium onions
seasoning
8 lamb's kidneys
175 g/6 oz puff pastry
little milk

Peel the onions, cut in half from top to bottom and remove most of the centre so that each onion becomes two shells, then season. Skin the kidneys, place one in each onion shell and sandwich the two onion halves together again.

Roll out the pastry very thinly and cut into 8 equal squares. Place each onion in the centre of each pastry square, gather the pastry corners to the top and seal firmly and glaze with milk. Bake on a greased baking sheet in first a hot, then a moderate oven.

TRIPE AND ONIONS

Cooking time 2 hours 20 minutes Serves 4

METRIC/IMPERIAL

900 g/2 lb tripe, cut into 5-cm/2-inch pieces
2 large onions, sliced
100 g/4 oz butter
300 ml/½ pint milk
300 ml/½ pint water
seasoning
150 ml/¼ pint single cream
1 tablespoon flour
chopped parsley to garnish

Blanch the tripe in boiling water, then drain. Sauté the onions in the butter, add the tripe, milk, water and a little salt. Simmer slowly for about 2 hours. Mix the cream and flour together, blend into the tripe and continue simmering for a further 20 minutes. Carefully season with pepper to taste, before serving sprinkled with chopped parsley.

LIVER ITALIAN

Cooking time 35 minutes Serves 4

METRIC/IMPERIAL

350–450 g/12 oz–1 lb lamb's liver, thinly sliced
seasoning
25 g/1 oz flour
15 g/½ oz butter
1 tablespoon oil
2 large onions, sliced
150 ml/¼ pint beef stock
2 tablespoons tomato purée
1 clove garlic, crushed
2 teaspoons basil
150 ml/¼ pint single cream
salt
freshly ground pepper
chopped parsley to garnish

Toss the sliced liver in the seasoned flour. Brown the liver in the butter and oil. Remove the liver and fry the onions until they are softened. Stir in the stock, tomato purée, garlic and basil, bring to the boil and return the liver to the pan. Cover and simmer slowly for about 25 minutes, until the liver is quite tender. When cooked, arrange the liver on a serving dish, add the cream to the sauce and adjust seasoning to taste. Reheat, but do not boil, pour over the liver and garnish with chopped parsley.

LEEK AND LIVER HOT-POT

Cooking time 2 hours Serves 4
Oven temperature Moderate 180°C, 350°F, Gas Mark 4

METRIC/IMPERIAL

450 g/1 lb leeks
225 g/8 oz tomatoes
8 rashers streaky bacon
450 g/1 lb lamb's liver, sliced
12 prunes, soaked
seasoning
450 ml/¾ pint stock

Prepare the leeks, peel the tomatoes and slice both thickly. Remove the bacon rind and roll up the rashers tightly. Layer the liver, leeks, tomatoes and prunes in a casserole dish, seasoning each layer. Pour over the stock to just cover the ingredients and top with the bacon rolls. Cover and cook for 1½ hours, then remove the lid and continue cooking for a further 30 minutes until the bacon is golden brown. Serve from the cooking dish.

Variations
Ox's liver may be used but it will take up to an hour longer.
Calf's liver may also be used, taking about one hour less.

ORANGEY LIVER

Cooking time few minutes Serves 3–4

METRIC/IMPERIAL

450 g/1 lb lamb's or pig's liver
1 tablespoon oil
40 g/1½ oz butter
2–3 shallots, finely chopped
1 clove garlic, crushed
seasoned flour
1 tablespoon orange juice
150 ml/¼ pint Dubonnet
2 tablespoons chopped parsley
grated rind of 1 orange
grated rind of 1 lemon

Slice the liver into about 1 cm/½ inch thick slices. Fry the shallots and garlic in the oil and butter until the shallots begin to brown. Toss the liver in the seasoned flour and fry gently taking care not to overcook. Remove the liver and keep it warm.

Add the orange juice and Dubonnet to the frying pan and bring to the boil, stirring all the time until the sauce has thickened. Add most of the grated rinds and chopped parsley (reserving the remainder for garnishing), bring the sauce to boiling point, pour it over the liver and serve.

FAGGOTS

Cooking time 50 minutes Serves 4
Oven temperature Moderate 180°C, 350°F, Gas Mark 4

METRIC/IMPERIAL

450 g/1 lb pig's liver
2 large onions
150 g/5 oz fresh white breadcrumbs
50 g/2 oz shredded suet
½ teaspoon dried sage
1 tablespoon Worcestershire sauce
seasoning

To serve
Espagnole Sauce (see page 175) or Tomato Sauce (see page 177).

Mince the liver and onions and mix together with all the other ingredients. Divide into eight portions and shape into balls. Bake on a greased ovenproof dish, turning over during cooking.

Pour over the sauce (or a good gravy) and return to the oven for a further 20 minutes.

LEEK AND LIVER SAUSAGE HOTPOT

Cooking time 1¼ hours Serves 4
Oven temperature Moderate 180°C, 350°F, Gas Mark 4

METRIC/IMPERIAL

675 g/1½ lb potatoes, peeled and thinly sliced
450 g/1 lb leeks, sliced
450 g/1 lb liver sausage (with skin removed), sliced
seasoning
225 g/8 oz streaky bacon (with rind removed), cut into thin strips
300 ml/½ pint stock

Arrange the potatoes, leeks and liver sausage in layers in a 1.75 litre/3-pint casserole, starting and finishing with a layer of potatoes and seasoning each layer well. Cover the top with bacon strips and pour in the stock. Cover and cook for approximately 40 minutes in a moderate oven. Remove the lid and cook for a further 30 minutes, until the potatoes are cooked and the bacon browned.

SAUSAGE SUPPER

Cooking time 1¼ hours Serves 4
Oven temperature Moderately hot 190°C, 375°F, Gas Mark 5

METRIC/IMPERIAL

675 g/1½ lb potatoes, thinly sliced
200 g/7 oz onions, thinly sliced
200 g/7 oz cooking apples, thinly sliced
2 tablespoons Worcestershire sauce
seasoning
450 g/1 lb chipolata sausages

Butter a 1.4 litre/2½ pint ovenproof dish. Layer the potatoes, onions and apples in the dish, beginning and ending with the potatoes. Season each layer with the Worcestershire sauce, salt and pepper and cover with a lid or foil. Bake for 45 minutes, then remove the foil. Arrange the sausages on top and return to the oven for a further 30 minutes until the sausages are cooked and the potatoes are golden brown.

GARDENER'S CASSEROLE

Cooking time 30–45 minutes Serves 4

METRIC/IMPERIAL

2 onions
1 leek
4 carrots
1 small cauliflower
50 g/2 oz butter
50 g/2 oz flour
1 litre/1¾ pint stock
1 tablespoon wine vinegar
450 g/1 lb spicy sausages, cooked and chopped
seasoning
50 g/2 oz Cheddar cheese, grated

Prepare the onions, leek, carrots and cauliflower. Chop the onions and leek, slice the carrots and break the cauliflower into small florets. Gently cook all the vegetables together in the butter for 15–20 minutes until they are soft but not mushy. Add the flour and cook for 2–3 minutes. Gradually add the stock, vinegar and sausages. Simmer for a further 15–20 minutes and season to taste. Place in an ovenproof serving dish; sprinkle with grated cheese just before serving. May be browned in a hot oven or under the grill.

Variations
Sausages may be freshly cooked English type or the pre-cooked Continental type.

SAUSAGE RISOTTO

Cooking time 30–40 minutes Serves 4

METRIC/IMPERIAL

12 skinless beef sausages
2 tablespoons cooking oil
1 large onion, chopped
225 g/8 oz long-grain rice
600 ml/1 pint stock (made from beef stock cube, pineapple juice and water)
75 g/3 oz mixed frozen vegetables
150 g/5 oz button mushrooms
1 green pepper, chopped
3 pineapple rings, chopped
seasoning

Cut each sausage in four. Fry them in the oil for about 5 minutes, until brown, then remove from the pan. Fry the onion and rice for a few minutes, add the stock and bring to the boil. Return sausages and all the other ingredients. Cover with a lid or foil and simmer for 30–40 minutes, until all the liquid is absorbed and the rice is cooked.

Variation
Sausages may be replaced by diced beefburger, cooked chicken, prawns; pineapple by peaches, apricots, apples; vegetables by celery, tomatoes, etc.

BEER SAUSAGE BAKE

Cooking time 15 minutes Serves 4
Oven temperature Moderately hot 200°C, 400°F, Gas Mark 6

METRIC/IMPERIAL

450 g/1 lb pork sausages
2 apples, peeled and cored
2 onions, sliced
1 tablespoon flour
300 ml/½ pint light ale
1 chicken stock cube
seasoning
1 packet instant potato (4–5 servings)

Brown the sausages for 5–10 minutes in a frying pan. Remove to an ovenproof dish. Cook the apples and onions in the sausage fat, until softened. Spoon over the sausages. Add the flour to about 1 tablespoon of the remaining fat in the pan. Add the light ale and stock cube, bring to the boil to thicken and season. Pour over the sausage mix. Make up the mashed potato as instructed and spread on top of the apples and onions, to cover completely. Bake in a moderately hot oven until the potato browns.

SWISS LEEK WITH SAUSAGE

Cooking time 1 hour Serves 4
Oven temperature Hot 220°C, 425°F, Gas Mark 7

METRIC/IMPERIAL

1 kg/2 lb leeks, chopped
3 large potatoes, peeled and sliced
450 ml/¾ pint stock
1 tablespoon flour
2 teaspoons milk
seasoning
thyme, basil, nutmeg
225 g/8 oz smoked bacon, in thick slices
225 g/8 oz smoked sausage, in one piece

Put the leeks and potatoes in an ovenproof dish, cover with the stock and simmer gently for 50 minutes. Blend the flour with the milk and stir into the vegetable mixture, adding the seasoning and herbs to taste. Poach the bacon and sausage for 8–10 minutes. Layer the bacon over the vegetables. Slice the sausage into eight pieces and layer down the centre of the dish.

Heat in a hot oven for about 10 minutes.

SAUSAGES IN ORANGE SAUCE

Cooking time 20 minutes Serves 4

METRIC/IMPERIAL

450 g/1 lb pork sausages
2 onions, thinly sliced
2 tablespoons vinegar
2 tablespoons redcurrant jelly
½ (178-ml/6¼-fl oz) can frozen orange juice
1 orange, peeled and sliced

Brown the sausages in a frying pan and pour away any excess fat. Add the onions, vinegar, redcurrant jelly and orange juice made up to 300 ml/½ pint with water. Simmer for 20 minutes. Serve garnished with fresh orange segments and creamed potatoes.

Variation
The orange sauce is also delicious with roast pork.

SPICY SAUSAGE IN CIDER

Cooking time 1 hour Serves 4
Oven temperature Moderate 180°C, 350°F, Gas Mark 4

METRIC/IMPERIAL

8 large pork sausages
seasoning
2 tablespoons flour
25 g/1 oz lard
2 apples, sliced and cored, but not peeled
4 shallots, finely chopped
3 cloves garlic, crushed
generous pinch chopped sage and parsley
300 ml/½ pint dry cider

Toss the sausages in the seasoned flour and fry them lightly in the fat. Place in a casserole dish with the apples, shallots, garlic and herbs. Add the cider and cover the dish with a lid or foil. Bake in a moderate oven for about an hour.

CHICKEN PIMENTO

Cooking time 50–60 minutes (depending on the size of the chicken joints) Serves 4
Oven temperature Moderately hot 190°C, 375°F, Gas Mark 5

METRIC/IMPERIAL

2 onions, sliced
25 g/1 oz butter
4 chicken portions
salt
black pepper
½ large red pepper
½ large green pepper
2 (150-g/5.3-oz) cartons natural yogurt
2 teaspoons paprika

Sauté the onions slowly in the butter and place in the base of an oven-proof dish. Place the chicken joints on top and season well. Slice the peppers thinly into rings, discarding the seeds. Cover the chicken with the pepper rings and the yogurt mixed with paprika. Bake until the chicken is tender.

TANDOORI-STYLE CHICKEN

Cooking time 30 minutes Serves 4–6

METRIC/IMPERIAL

1.5 kg/3½ lb roasting chicken

Marinade

2 (150-g/5.3-oz) cartons natural yogurt
½ teaspoon ground ginger
1 tablespoon paprika
1 tablespoon chilli
1 clove garlic, crushed
4 bay leaves
6 peppercorns
1 tablespoon tomato purée
grated rind of 1 lemon
1 teaspoon salt

Kebabs

8 shallots, skinned
1 large green pepper
1 medium red pepper
2 lemons, cut into wedges
100 g/4 oz button mushrooms

Skin and bone the chicken and chop the chicken pieces into about 5-cm/2-inch pieces. Place the chicken in the marinade and leave covered in the refrigerator for 24 hours.

To make the kebabs, simmer the shallots for 10 minutes. Slice the peppers thickly, discarding the seeds, and blanch the slices for 1 minute. Thread the chicken, shallots, peppers, lemon and mushrooms alternately on to 4–6 skewers. Place under a moderate grill for about 15–20 minutes, turning occasionally, basting with the marinade, until the chicken is cooked.

CHICKEN IN A PARCEL

Cooking time 1 hour Serves 1
Oven temperature Hot 220°C, 425°F, Gas Mark 7

METRIC/IMPERIAL

1 chicken portion
25 g/1 oz butter
2–3 mushrooms
2–3 baby onions
2 tablespoons single cream or top of milk
1 tablespoon sherry
seasoning

Brown the chicken portion in the butter in a frying pan. Place the chicken with all the other ingredients on a piece of foil, parcel up loosely and bake in a hot oven for 1 hour.

QUICK CHICKEN PROVENÇAL

Cooking time 1 hour Serves 4
Oven temperature Moderately hot 190°C, 375°F, Gas Mark 5

METRIC/IMPERIAL

450 g/1 lb canned spaghetti rings
450 g/1 lb canned tomatoes
1 large onion, chopped
1 teaspoon sugar
½ teaspoon basil
4 chicken portions
seasoning
1 wineglass dry sherry (optional)

Lay the spaghetti rings in a 1.5 litre/2½ pint shallow ovenproof dish. Mix the tomatoes, onion, sugar and basil and place on the spaghetti. Place the chicken portions on top and season well. Cover with a lid or foil and bake in a moderately hot oven for 45 minutes. Remove the lid or foil, add the sherry and bake for 15 minutes to crisp the skin.

ROAST GARLIC CHICKEN

Cooking time 1½–2 hours Serves 6
Oven temperature Moderately hot 200°C, 400°F, Gas Mark 6

METRIC/IMPERIAL

1 large onion, finely chopped
seasoning
50 g/2 oz fresh white breadcrumbs
2 tablespoons chopped parsley
½ teaspoon thyme (fresh or dried)
grated rind ½ lemon
50 g/2 oz garlic sausage, finely chopped
1 egg, beaten
1 (1.5-kg/3½-lb) oven-ready chicken
40 g/1½ oz margarine or butter
2 tablespoons flour
2 chicken stock cubes plus 400 ml/14 fl oz hot water
2 tablespoons lemon juice

Combine the onion, seasoning, breadcrumbs, herbs, lemon rind and garlic sausage and bind together with the beaten egg. Use to stuff the neck end of the chicken. Secure and truss the chicken well. Season the bird well and dot with the margarine or butter. Roast in a moderately hot oven for 1½–1¾ hours until the chicken is cooked, golden brown and tender – baste during cooking. Remove the chicken to a serving dish and make a sauce with the flour, stock, lemon juice and pan juices. Season to taste and simmer for 2–3 minutes before serving with the chicken.

AMERICAN CHICKEN SALAD

Cooking time 25–35 minutes Serves 4
Oven temperature Hot 230°C, 450°F, Gas Mark 8

METRIC/IMPERIAL

400 g/14 oz cooked chicken (or turkey)
2 (300-g/10½-oz) cans condensed chicken soup
2 cups celery, chopped
1 small onion, finely chopped
1 cup walnuts, chopped
1 teaspoon salt
1 teaspoon pepper
2 tablespoons lemon juice
1½ cups mayonnaise (see page 180)
4 hard-boiled eggs, roughly chopped
4 cups potato crisps, crushed
chopped parsley to garnish

Note Cup measure approximately 250 ml/ 8 fl oz. These are used because proportions of one ingredient to another in volume are more important than the exact weights.

If the meat is on the carcass, remove and cut into medium pieces. Combine all the ingredients, except the potato crisps and parsley. Place in a shallow 1.5 litre/2½ pint ovenproof dish and cover with a lid or foil. Bake in a hot oven for 20–30 minutes. Remove the lid or foil. Cover with the crushed potato crisps and return to the oven for about 5 minutes, until the crisps begin to brown. Garnish with the chopped parsley.

HAWAIIAN CHICKEN

Cooking time 10–15 minutes Serves 4

METRIC/IMPERIAL

1 fresh pineapple
1 onion, chopped
1 green pepper, seeded and chopped
25 g/1 oz butter
150 ml/¼ pint stock or water
225 g/8 oz cooked chicken
2 teaspoons brown sugar
1 tablespoon vinegar
2 teaspoons soy sauce
2 teaspoons cornflour
seasoning

Slice the pineapple in half lengthways. Scoop out the pineapple flesh, reserving as much juice as possible, and chop finely. Fry the onion and pepper gently in the butter. Add the pineapple juice, made up to 250 ml/8 fl oz with stock or water. Cut the cooked chicken into medium pieces and add to the pan with the sugar, vinegar and soy sauce. Blend the cornflour to a paste with a little water and stir into the pan to thicken the sauce, then season to taste. Divide the mixture between the pineapple shells and serve on boiled rice.

NORWEGIAN HOT POT

Cooking time 15–20 minutes Serves 4–6
Oven temperature Hot 230°C, 450°F, Gas Mark 8

METRIC/IMPERIAL

450 g/1 lb cooked chicken
175 g/6 oz cooked ham
175 g/6 oz cooked roast beef
275 g/10 oz cooked peas
2 leeks, cooked and cut into 2.5-cm/1-inch pieces
4 tomatoes, peeled and quartered
15 g/½ oz butter
2 tablespoons flour
450 ml/¾ pint beef stock
salt
freshly ground black pepper
1 teaspoon soy sauce
5 tablespoons Madeira

Cut the chicken, ham and beef into 2.5 cm/1 inch pieces. Put all the meat and vegetables into an ovenproof casserole. Melt the butter, add the flour and cook to a brown roux. Add the stock and bring to the boil, stirring, for 3–4 minutes. Season to taste with the salt, pepper and soy sauce. Add the Madeira. Pour this sauce over the meat and vegetables and heat the whole dish through thoroughly in a hot oven for about 15 minutes.

RABBIT SAUTÉ

Cooking time 1½–2 hours Serves 4
Oven temperature Moderate 180°C, 350°F, Gas Mark 4

METRIC/IMPERIAL

1 rabbit
75 g/3 oz bacon fat or butter or oil
3 onions, chopped
3 carrots, chopped
50 g/2 oz flour
300 ml/½ pint stock
300 ml/½ pint white wine
50 g/2 oz tomato purée
1 clove garlic, crushed
bouquet garni
seasoning

To garnish
chopped parsley
chopped chives

Divide the rabbit into about 8 pieces and brown these on all sides in hot fat. Remove the rabbit pieces to an ovenproof dish. Fry the vegetables in the remaining fat, stir in the flour and add the stock, wine, purée, garlic, bouquet garni and seasoning to taste. Pour over the rabbit and cook in a moderate oven until the rabbit is tender. Sprinkle with the parsley and chives before serving.

POACHER'S PIE

Cooking time 2 hours Serves 4
Oven temperature Hot 220°C, 425°F, Gas Mark 7 – 30 minutes
Moderate 160°C, 325°F, Gas Mark 3 – 1½ hours

METRIC/IMPERIAL

675 g/1½ lb rabbit
350 g/12 oz belly pork
25 g/1 oz seasoned flour
2 large onions, sliced
2 carrots, sliced
2 tablespoons chopped parsley
seasoning
300 ml/½ pint chicken stock
3 tablespoons Worcestershire sauce
1 (213-g/7½-oz) packet frozen puff pastry
beaten egg for glaze

Cut the rabbit into 8 pieces and the belly pork into cubes. Coat the rabbit and pork well with the seasoned flour. Arrange the meats, vegetables and parsley in layers in a 1 litre/1¾ pint pie dish, seasoning each layer. Pour over the stock and Worcestershire sauce. Roll out the thawed pastry to cover the pie. Brush with the egg. Bake as above, covering the pie with foil when the oven temperature is reduced.

Onion Accompaniments

Although I have covered the basic cooking methods of the onion family of vegetables elsewhere in this book, they all lend themselves extremely well to special treatment. Although, for convenience, these recipes are grouped together as accompaniments, many of them can stand on their own as excellent starters or as separate vegetable courses.

CRISPY ONION CIRCLES

Cooking time few minutes Makes approx 12–14 rings and centres

METRIC/IMPERIAL

50 g/2 oz fat
100 g/4 oz flour
2 tablespoons water
1 large onion, finely chopped
1 egg
2 tablespoons milk
breadcrumbs
oil for deep frying

Rub the fat into the flour until the mixture resembles fine breadcrumbs. Add the water and chopped onion to make a stiff dough. Roll out the pastry to about 5 mm/¼ inch thick and cut out rings using first a 6 cm/2½ inch cutter and then a 3.5 cm/1½ inch cutter to cut out the centres. Roll out the trimmings and centres and cut out more rings until all the pastry is used. Dip the rings into the beaten egg and milk and then into the breadcrumbs. Deep fry, not too quickly, until they are golden brown. Drain on kitchen paper. Eat hot.

Variation
Brush the removed centre circles with the egg and milk glaze and place on a greased baking sheet and bake in a moderate oven 180°C, 350°F, Gas Mark 4 for 15 minutes.

GLAZED ONIONS

Cooking time 10–15 minutes Serves 4

METRIC/IMPERIAL

450 g/1 lb button onions
25 g/1 oz sugar
50 g/2 oz butter

Bring a pan of salted water to the boil and drop in the unpeeled baby onions; simmer for 5–7 minutes. Drain, peel, rinse under cold water and dab dry.

Melt the sugar and butter in a heavy-based frying pan, without browning. Add the onions and toss continually for 5–6 minutes until they are caramelized and evenly coated. This dish is particularly good with bacon, roast meats and game.

LEEKS WITH RICE

Cooking time 30–35 minutes Serves 4

METRIC/IMPERIAL

4 tablespoons olive oil
1 clove garlic, crushed
450 g/1 lb leeks, sliced
2 tablespoons tomato purée
1 teaspoon sugar
1 tablespoon lemon juice
1 teaspoon mixed herbs
salt
freshly ground black pepper
scant 450 ml/¾ pint water or chicken stock
225 g/8 oz long-grain rice, washed

Heat the oil in a large saucepan, add the garlic and cook over a low heat for 1 minute. Add the leeks and cook, stirring, for 5 minutes. Stir in the tomato purée, sugar, lemon juice, herbs and seasoning. Add the water or stock and bring to the boil. Reduce the heat, cover the pan and simmer for 10 minutes or until the leeks are nearly tender. Add the rice, bring to the boil and stir with a fork to separate the grains of rice. Adjust seasoning. Cover the pan, reduce the heat and simmer gently for 15–20 minutes, until the rice is cooked and all the liquid has been absorbed.

Serve as an accompaniment to grilled chops, steak or sausages.

LEEKS WITH RED WINE

Cooking time 10 minutes Serves 2

METRIC/IMPERIAL

450 g/1 lb small leeks
3–4 tablespoons oil
salt
1 wineglass dry red wine
2 tablespoons stock or water

Clean the leeks and cut away most of the green part (save this and use for soup). Heat the oil in a shallow pan, put in the leeks side by side and cook gently until lightly coloured. Season with a *little* salt and pour over the wine. Add the stock or water. Cover the pan and cook for 7–10 minutes or until the leeks are tender, turning them over once. Put the leeks into a shallow dish to keep hot. Reduce the sauce by boiling rapidly and pour over the leeks.

BRAISED LEEKS

Cooking time 20 minutes Serves 4

METRIC/IMPERIAL

675 g/1½ lb leeks
600 ml/1 pint chicken stock
1 bouquet garni
75 g/3 oz butter
seasoning
chopped parsley to garnish

Wash the leeks, trim and remove only the upper parts of the leaves. Place in a wide saucepan, with just sufficient stock to cover. Add the bouquet garni and butter. Season carefully, the amount depending on the flavour of the stock used. Bring to the boil, cover the leeks with greaseproof paper and a lid. Simmer until the leeks are tender, by which time most of the stock will have evaporated. Place the leeks on a serving dish and remove the bouquet garni. Reduce the juices in the pan by boiling rapidly. Pour over the leeks and garnish with parsley.

LEEKS IN SOURED CREAM

Cooking time 30–40 minutes Serves 4
Oven temperature Moderate 180°C, 350°F, Gas Mark 4

METRIC/IMPERIAL

8 young leeks
200 ml/7 fl oz chicken stock
grated rind and juice of ½ lemon
20 g/¾ oz margarine
20 g/¾ oz flour
1 (142-ml/5-fl oz) carton soured cream
seasoning
chopped parsley to garnish

Cut the leeks through in half lengthways and wash thoroughly, then blanch in boiling salted water for 5 minutes. Place the leeks in a shallow ovenproof dish and pour over the chicken stock and lemon rind and juice. Cover the dish and bake for 20–30 minutes, until tender. Strain off the liquid, reserving 150 ml/¼ pint and mix this with the margarine and flour, whisking together to make a smooth sauce. Cook for 2–3 minutes, add the soured cream, check the seasoning and reheat gently before pouring over the leeks. Garnish with chopped parsley before serving.

LEEKS IN CREAM

Cooking time 10–15 minutes Serves 4
(as an accompanying vegetable)
Oven temperature Moderately hot 190°C, 375°F, Gas Mark 5

METRIC/IMPERIAL

4–6 leeks
6 tablespoons single cream
seasoning
2 tablespoons fresh breadcrumbs
20 g/¾ oz butter

Clean the leeks well, cut into about 10 cm/4 inch slices, then cut in half lengthways. Cook in boiling salted water until just tender. Drain thoroughly, pressing the water out well. Place in a buttered ovenproof dish. Pour over the cream and seasoning, scatter the breadcrumbs on top and dot with the butter. Brown the topping in a moderately hot oven or under the grill.

CRISPY-COATED LEEKS

Cooking time about 15–20 minutes Serves 4

METRIC/IMPERIAL

8 leeks
salt
1 egg, beaten
3–4 tablespoons breadcrumbs
50 g/2 oz butter (or oil for deep frying)

Prepare and cook the leeks in salted water until just tender, about 15 minutes (see page 29). Drain very well on kitchen paper. Dip the leeks in the beaten egg and then the breadcrumbs, to give a thick coating. Allow to firm up for about an hour in the refrigerator, before shallow or deep-fat frying until crisp and golden brown. Drain on absorbent kitchen paper.

CHINESE LEEKS

Cooking time 10 minutes Serves 4

METRIC/IMPERIAL

1 kg/2 lb leeks, trimmed, washed and halved
4 tablespoons vinegar
1 tablespoon oil
2 tablespoons tomato ketchup
1 tablespoon soy sauce
1 tablespoon honey
1 tablespoon brown sugar
seasoning
50 g/2 oz sultanas

Prepare the leeks (as page 29), simmer until tender for 5–8 minutes, according to their thickness. Drain well and transfer to a serving dish. Mix all the remaining ingredients gently together in a saucepan over low heat until the sugar and honey have dissolved. Spoon over the leeks and chill for at least an hour before serving.

SPRING ONIONS À LA KING

Cooking time 20 minutes Serves 4

METRIC/IMPERIAL

36 good-sized spring onions
seasoning
1 green pepper, seeded and thinly sliced
4 hard-boiled eggs
40 g/1½ oz butter
40 g/1½ oz flour
450 ml/¾ pint milk
4 tablespoons cooked sweet corn
garlic croûtons to garnish (see page 139)

Prepare the spring onions, leaving about 2.5 cm/1 inch of green. Cook in well-seasoned boiling water until just tender, add the sliced pepper and cook for a further 5 minutes. Drain well. Shell and slice the hard-boiled eggs.

Make a white sauce with the butter, flour and milk (see page 173). Gently mix the eggs, sweetcorn and spring onion mixture together, place in a heated serving dish, pour over the sauce and garnish with the garlic croûtons.

CHIVES AND CUCUMBER – HOT

Cooking time 5 minutes Serves 4

METRIC/IMPERIAL

2 cucumbers
1 tablespoon chopped chives
300 ml/½ pint white sauce (see page 173)
seasoning

Peel the cucumbers, cut into cubes and blanch in boiling water for 3–4 minutes. Drain well. Add the chives and seasoning to the white sauce, pour over the cucumber, heat through and serve.

ONION AND COURGETTE BAKE

Cooking time 15 minutes Serves 4
(as an accompanying vegetable)
Oven temperature Hot 220°C, 425°F, Gas Mark 7

METRIC/IMPERIAL

450 g/1 lb courgettes, grated
1 large onion, finely chopped
50 g/2 oz Cheddar cheese, grated

Combine the courgettes and onion and place in a lightly buttered shallow ovenproof dish. Sprinkle the cheese on top and bake until nicely browned.

Variations
The courgettes may be stir-fried with the onion on top of the stove, a good method for those rather too large courgettes.

CABBAGE WITH ONION

Cooking time 7–8 minutes Serves 4

METRIC/IMPERIAL

1 small hard white cabbage
2 teaspoons salt
50 g/2 oz butter
1 onion
freshly ground black pepper

Shred the cabbage finely, sprinkle with salt, cover with cold water and leave for 10 minutes, then drain. Melt half the butter in a large saucepan, add the cabbage and cook in the covered pan, shaking regularly to prevent sticking, for about 5 minutes. Meanwhile, fry the onion in the remaining butter until slightly browned. Combine with the cooked cabbage and cook for a further two minutes. Serve with plenty of black pepper.

TOMATO AND ONION CASSEROLE

Cooking time 45 minutes Serves 4
Oven temperature Moderate 180°C, 350°F, Gas Mark 4

METRIC/IMPERIAL

1 large onion, chopped
50 g/2 oz butter
4 ripe tomatoes, peeled and sliced
12 tablespoons grated cheese
12 tablespoons soft white breadcrumbs
12 tablespoons soured cream
2 eggs
seasoning
½ teaspoon basil

Cook the onions in the butter until tender. Place half the tomatoes in a greased ovenproof dish. Top with a layer of onions, cheese and crumbs. Repeat layers of the ingredients until the dish is full, ending with the crumb topping. Mix the soured cream, eggs, seasoning and basil together and pour over the vegetables. Cover the dish and bake for 30 minutes, then uncover and bake for a further 10 minutes to brown the topping.

BRAISED CELERY WITH ONIONS AND WALNUTS

Cooking time 20 minutes Serves 4

METRIC/IMPERIAL

1 head celery, cut into 1-cm/½-inch strips
2 onions, finely chopped
25 g/1 oz butter or margarine
150 ml/¼ pint chicken stock
seasoning
50 g/2 oz walnuts, chopped
chopped parsley to garnish

Bring the celery to the boil in salted water, drain and dab dry with kitchen paper. Sauté the onions and celery together in the butter for 5–7 minutes until soft. Add the stock and seasoning and simmer for about 10 minutes. Add the walnuts and toss into the mixture just to heat through before turning into a serving dish. Garnish with a sprinkling of chopped parsley.

SPICY CAULIFLOWER

Cooking time 25 minutes Serves 4

METRIC/IMPERIAL

1 large cauliflower, broken into florets
1 onion, finely chopped
25 g/1 oz margarine or butter
15 g/½ oz flour
1 curry stock cube dissolved in 300 ml/½ pint water
seasoning
1 (150-g/5.3-oz) carton natural yogurt or soured cream
few salted nuts, chopped
paprika

Blanch the cauliflower in boiling salted water for 10 minutes, then drain. Sauté the onion in the fat until soft, about 5 minutes. Add the flour and curry stock and cook for 2–3 minutes until smooth and the sauce has thickened. Season to taste. Add the cauliflower, simmer for about 7–10 minutes until just tender and stir in the yogurt or cream carefully. Serve topped with a sprinkling of nuts and paprika.

SPROUTS WITH ONIONS

Cooking time 10–15 minutes Serves 4

METRIC/IMPERIAL

450 g/1 lb Brussels sprouts
2 tablespoons finely chopped onion
15 g/½ oz butter
1 tablespoon flour
2 teaspoons brown sugar
½ teaspoons salt
½ teaspoon dry mustard
150 ml/¼ pint milk
150 ml/¼ pint soured cream
fried croûtons to garnish

Cook the spouts until tender. Sauté the onion in the butter, not allowing it to brown. Stir in the flour, sugar, salt and mustard and cook for about one minute. Add the milk gradually and make a sauce. Remove from heat and add the soured cream. Drain the sprouts well, combine with the sauce and reheat, but do not allow to boil. Serve in a warmed dish, garnished with croûtons.

PAPRIKA BEANS

Cooking time 15–20 minutes Serves 4

METRIC/IMPERIAL

450 g/1 lb French beans
50 g/2 oz butter
1 large onion, finely chopped
1 tablespoon paprika
2 tablespoons flour
150 ml/¼ pint single cream
seasoning

Cook the beans in boiling salted water until they are only just tender; strain. Melt the butter and fry the onion gently until transparent. Remove from the heat and add the paprika. Blend the flour with the cream and add to the onion mixture, stirring all the time. Cook on a low heat for 5 minutes. Add the beans and seasoning and simmer for 5 minutes before serving.

BROAD BEANS WITH YOGURT

Cooking time 10–15 minutes Serves 4

METRIC/IMPERIAL

2 tablespoons long-grain rice
350 g/12 oz broad beans, cooked
1 clove garlic, crushed
1 (150-g/5.3-oz) carton natural yogurt
seasoning
1 egg, beaten

Cook the rice in boiling salted water for 10 minutes. Strain the beans and rice and mix together while they are still hot. Stir the garlic into the yogurt. Add seasoning and yogurt to the beans and rice and heat through gently. Add the beaten egg and stir over a low heat until the sauce thickens. Serve hot or cold.

HOT VEGETABLE SLAW

Cooking time 20–25 minutes Serves 4

METRIC/IMPERIAL

1 large onion, thinly sliced
2 sticks celery, chopped
25 g/1 oz butter
3 carrots, grated
450 g/1 lb white cabbage, finely shredded
1 tablespoon Worcestershire sauce
seasoning

Fry the onion and celery gently in the butter for about 5 minutes. Add all the remaining ingredients, cover with a well-fitting lid and cook gently for a further 15–20 minutes, shaking the pan frequently, until the vegetables are just tender. Serve immediately.

RATATOUILLE

Cooking time 45–55 minutes Serves 4
Oven temperature Moderate 180°C, 350°F, Gas Mark 4

METRIC/IMPERIAL

1 large aubergine, sliced
seasoning
1 large onion, sliced
2 cloves garlic, crushed
40 g/1½ oz butter or margarine
1 green pepper, seeded and sliced
2 courgettes, sliced
1 tablespoon tomato purée
350 g/12 oz tomatoes, peeled and thickly sliced
pinch basil, oregano and marjoram
chopped parsley
2 teaspoons sugar
1 teaspoon Worcestershire sauce

Sprinkle the sliced aubergine with salt and leave for 30 minutes, drain and dry. Sauté the onion and garlic in the butter for 5 minutes, add the pepper and continue cooking for 2–3 minutes before adding the aubergine, courgettes and tomato purée. Cook for a further 5 minutes. Stir in the sliced tomatoes and herbs, sugar, Worcestershire sauce and seasoning to taste. Place in an ovenproof dish with about 2 tablespoons of water in a moderate oven until all the flavours have mingled together, about 30–40 minutes.

May be served hot or cold, as an hors d'oeuvre or as an accompanying vegetable.

POTATOES MEXICANO

Cooking time 1 hour Serves 4
Oven temperature Moderately hot 190°C, 375°F, Gas Mark 5

METRIC/IMPERIAL

450–675 g/1–1½ lb potatoes, thinly sliced
1 large onion, coarsely grated
1 (198-g/7-oz) can sweet corn with peppers
seasoning
300 ml/½ pint chicken stock
50 g/2 oz bacon, diced
15 g/½ oz butter or margarine
2–3 tablespoons double cream

Layer the potatoes, onion and sweet corn in a greased ovenproof dish, seasoning well between each layer, beginning and ending with a layer of potatoes. Pour over the stock and bake in a moderately hot oven for 45 minutes. Sauté the bacon in the butter. Add the bacon to the lightly whipped cream, pour the mixture on to the potato and bake for a further 15 minutes, until browned.

NORMANDY POTATOES

Cooking time 40 minutes Serves 4–6

METRIC/IMPERIAL

1 large onion, finely chopped
1 leek, finely chopped
150 g/5 oz bacon, chopped
50 g/2 oz butter
1 kg/2¼ lb potatoes, thinly sliced
150 ml/¼ pint chicken stock
300 ml/½ pint milk
seasoning

To garnish
paprika
parsley

Sauté the onion, leek and bacon in the butter for one minute to soften. Add the sliced potatoes, stock and milk. Season well and simmer for approximately 30–40 minutes until the potatoes are tender. Serve garnished with the paprika and chopped parsley.

GARLIC POTATOES

Cooking time 15 minutes Serves 4

METRIC/IMPERIAL

675 g/1½ lb cooked potatoes
3 tablespoons oil
1 onion, chopped
1 clove garlic, crushed
little salt

Cut the potatoes into slices or cubes, not so thinly that they break up. Fry the potatoes in the oil until they begin to brown. Add the onion, garlic and salt and continue frying until well browned.

SWISS POTATOES AND ONIONS

Cooking time 25 minutes (plus cooking time for potatoes)
Serves 4

METRIC/IMPERIAL

450 g/1 lb potatoes
1 large onion, finely chopped
seasoning
50 g/2 oz butter
1 tablespoon oil

Par-boil the potatoes in their skins so that they are still quite firm. Cool, skin and grate them coarsely. Mix with the onion and seasoning. Heat the butter and oil together in a large frying pan, place the potato mixture in the pan and spread over the base evenly. Cook gently for 10–15 minutes without disturbing, until the underside has browned. Turn the 'potato cake' over completely and cook the reverse side until browned for a further 10 minutes.

Serve as a flat cake, cutting in wedges to serve.

POTATO-CREAM BAKE

Cooking time 45 minutes Serves 4
Oven temperature Moderate 180°C, 350°F, Gas Mark 4

METRIC/IMPERIAL

6 medium potatoes
3 medium onions, finely chopped
50 g/2 oz butter
salt
freshly ground pepper
150 ml/¼ pint single cream
150 ml/¼ pint milk

Peel the potatoes and cut into very thin slices. Brown the onions in three-quarters of the butter. Place layers of potatoes and onions in a buttered 1 litre/1¾ pint ovenproof dish, ending with potato. Sprinkle with salt and pepper and dot with the remaining butter. Mix the cream with the milk and pour half over the dish. Bake in a moderate oven until the potatoes are cooked. Fifteen minutes before removing from the oven pour on the remaining cream mixture.

SOY RICE

Cooking time few minutes Serves 2

METRIC/IMPERIAL

60–75g/2–3 oz long grain rice
1 onion, finely chopped
2 tablespoons olive oil
seasoning
1 tablespoon soy sauce
2 eggs, beaten

Cook rice in boiling salted water for 10 minutes only. Rinse and drain. Heat the oil and fry the onion slowly until just tender. Add the rice and seasoning and fry gently, turning over constantly. Add the soy sauce to the beaten eggs and pour over the rice, continuing stirring until the rice is dry and the egg is cooked. Serve at once.

Salads

Fortunately the limp lettuce and whole tomato which years ago represented the British salad has almost disappeared, due perhaps to the enthusiastic and imaginative interpretation of salads by our Continental and American friends.

It may be that slimming too has had some influence, or the new interest in so-called health or natural foods, or even the increase in home gardening.

Whether or not you are already a salad enthusiast, I hope these recipes will add new interest to your salad making.

MRS BEETON'S ONION SALAD

Serves 5–6

METRIC/IMPERIAL

450 g/1 lb large mild onions
2–3 tablespoons French dressing (see page 181)
1 tablespoon finely chopped parsley

Peel the onions, cover with cold water, bring to the boil and then drain. Leave them in cold water for 6–7 hours, changing the water regularly. Slice thinly into a serving dish, pour over the French dressing and toss the onion slices gently. Serve garnished with chopped parsley.

ONIONS À LA GRECQUE

Cooking time 45 minutes Serves 4

METRIC/IMPERIAL

350 g/12 oz small button onions
225 g/8 oz tomatoes
2 wine glasses white wine
3 tablespoons olive oil
seasoning
1 teaspoon fennel, chopped (or ½ teaspoon dried fennel)
1 teaspoon coriander seeds
chopped parsley to garnish

Peel the onions carefully to leave them whole and undamaged. Peel and seed the tomatoes and chop the flesh. Blanch the onions for about 5–7 minutes, drain and return them to the saucepan with the tomatoes, wine, oil, seasoning, fennel and coriander. Cover and simmer for 45 minutes. Remove to a serving dish and serve well chilled, garnished with chopped parsley.

ONION AND CHEESE SALAD

Serves 4

METRIC/IMPERIAL

100 g/4 oz cheese
100 g/4 oz cooked ham
1 green pepper, seeded and cut into strips
1 large onion, thinly sliced
3 tablespoons French dressing (see page 181)
seasoning
lettuce leaves

Cut the cheese and ham into strips and combine with the pepper and onion. Toss lightly in the French dressing, seasoning to taste. Chill and serve piled on to lettuce leaves.

ONION AND GRAPEFRUIT SALAD

Serves 4

METRIC/IMPERIAL

2 large grapefruit
2 medium onions
4 tablespoons French dressing (see page 181)
chopped parsley to garinsh

Segment the grapefruit, peel and chop the onion finely. Toss in the salad dressing and serve in a shallow dish, sprinkled with the chopped parsley.

Variations
This is a good salad for fish, particularly firm oily fish like smoked mackerel.

The mixture may be returned to the grapefruit half shells and served as a starter for a rich meal to follow. Spring onions may also be used.

LEEK AND APPLE SALAD

Serves 4

METRIC/IMPERIAL

2 young leeks (white part only)
4 small cooking apples
1 tablespoon lemon juice
4 tomatoes, peeled
2 teaspoons sugar
4 tablespoons mayonnaise (see page 180)
chopped parsley to garnish

Trim the leeks, leaving only the white part, and then slice very thinly. Peel, core and slice the apples and sprinkle with the lemon juice. Slice the peeled tomatoes, sprinkling with the sugar. Mix all the ingredients together with the mayonnaise. Serve garnished with chopped parsley.

LEEK AND SHRIMP SALAD

Cooking time 10 minutes Serves 4

METRIC/IMPERIAL

8–12 young leeks, prepared
salt
1–2 tablespoons top of milk or single cream
300 ml/½ pint mayonnaise (see page 180)
100 g/4 oz shrimps or prawns
2 hard-boiled eggs
pepper
lemon juice
paprika

Tie the leeks into two bundles with string. Plunge into boiling salted water and cook until just tender, about 10 minutes. Lift out of the pan, remove the string and drain thoroughly on a clean cloth. Mix a little milk or cream with the mayonnaise, to thin to a coating consistency. Add the shrimps or prawns. Shell the eggs and remove the yolks from the whites. Shred the whites and add to the mayonnaise. Season with salt, pepper and lemon juice. Arrange the leeks in a serving dish and coat with the sauce. Sieve the yolks of the eggs over the top and dust with paprika.

CHICKEN SALAMAGUNDY

Serves 6–8

METRIC/IMPERIAL

- 150 ml/¼ pint double or whipping cream
- 150 ml/¼ pint mayonnaise (see page 180)
- 1 tablespoon chopped parsley
- 1 bunch spring onions
- 1 kg/2 lb cooked chicken meat
- 1 lemon
- seasoning
- 2 hard-boiled eggs
- 1 lettuce
- 150 ml/¼ pint French dressing (see page 181)
- 1 bunch radishes
- ½ cucumber, sliced
- 1 bunch watercress

Whip the cream until it is just thick and stir into the mayonnaise with the parsley and 1 tablespoon chopped spring onions. Slice the breast meat of the chicken into strips and dice any brown meat. Peel the lemon and chop the inside flesh. Mix it with the diced and sliced chicken and add to the mayonnaise and cream mixture. Season well. Pile in the centre of a large platter. Chop the egg whites and sieve the egg yolks and use to decorate the chicken mixture. Surround the chicken mixture with shredded lettuce, tossed in French dressing. Place radishes, cucumber and watercress around the dish for decoration.

GREEN SALAD WITH BLUE CHEESE DRESSING

Serves 4

METRIC/IMPERIAL

- 1 clove garlic
- 1 lettuce heart, torn into pieces
- 4 spring onions, chopped
- ½ cucumber, chopped
- 1 stick celery, chopped
- 1 green pepper, seeded and chopped
- 2 tablespoons chopped parsley
- 2 tablespoons chopped chives

Blue Cheese Dressing

- 100 g/4 oz blue-veined cheese
- 2 tablespoons wine vinegar
- 6 tablespoons olive oil
- 1 teaspoon French mustard

Rub a salad bowl with the garlic, before putting in all the salad ingredients. Blend all the dressing ingredients together in a bowl, until it is well mixed and smooth. Pour over the salad when ready to serve and toss well.

YORKSHIRE SALAD

Serves 4

METRIC/IMPERIAL

1 lettuce
1 bunch spring onions
1 tablespoon fresh chopped mint
1 clove garlic
sugar and vinegar to taste

Finely shred the lettuce and spring onions and add with chopped mint to a salad bowl which has been rubbed with the garlic clove. Add a little sugar and vinegar and toss and serve.

TOMATO SALAD

Serves 4

METRIC/IMPERIAL

4 large tomatoes
2 small onions
French dressing (see page 181)
chopped parsley or chives

Peel the tomatoes and slice crossways from the stalk end. Skin and finely slice the onions.

Place layers of the tomatoes and onions in a shallow salad bowl and cover with the dressing. Chill before serving garnished with chopped parsley or chives.

SWEET CORN AND SPRING ONION SALAD

Serves 6

METRIC/IMPERIAL

2 (326-g/11½-oz) cans sweet corn
2 bunches spring onions, chopped
French dressing (see page 181)
seasoning

Drain the cans of sweet corn thoroughly, place in a mixing bowl and mix with the chopped spring onions. Toss well in the French dressing and check seasoning to taste. Serve well chilled. This salad is good with cold chicken.

COURGETTE AND LEEK SALAD

Cooking time 5 minutes Serves 4

METRIC/IMPERIAL

2 tablespoons corn oil
1 tablespoon white vinegar
1 teaspoon fresh mixed herbs
1 teaspoon chopped chives
onion salt
salt
freshly ground black pepper
350 g/12 oz courgettes, wiped and trimmed
275 g/10 leeks, washed and thinly sliced

Put the oil, vinegar, herbs and seasoning into a screw-topped jar. Shake well and leave to infuse for 30 minutes.

Slice the courgettes 5 mm/¼ inch thick and blanch in boiling water until tender but still crisp, about 2 minutes. Drain and pat dry. Blanch the leeks in boiling water for about 2 minutes, drain well and add to the courgettes. Shake the dressing and pour over the vegetables whilst they are still warm. Toss lightly. Chill before serving.

CALIFORNIAN POTATO SALAD

Serves 4

METRIC/IMPERIAL

450 g/1 lb potatoes
4 tablespoons vinegar
1 teaspoon salt
1 large onion, chopped
pepper (to taste)
2 hard-boiled eggs
150 ml/¼ pint mayonnaise (see page 180)
1 tablespoon chopped parsley to garnish

Boil the potatoes in their skins. When cold peel, slice and dice them. Add the vinegar, mix and allow it to soak into the potatoes. Add the salt to the chopped onion and allow it to stand for 15 minutes. Squeeze out the juices and rinse the onion with cold water. Dry on absorbent paper and then add to the potatoes. Mix in the other ingredients and chill well.

Serve sprinkled with the chopped parsley.

PEPPER SLAW

Serves 4–6

METRIC/IMPERIAL

½ hard white cabbage, finely shredded
1 green pepper, thinly sliced
1 red pepper, thinly sliced
1 bunch spring onions, chopped
1 bunch radishes, sliced
2–3 tablespoons French dressing (see page 181)
6–8 tablespoons mayonnaise (see page 180)
1 teaspoon horseradish sauce
seasoning
chopped parsley to garnish

Mix together all the prepared vegetables in a large bowl. Add the French dressing and allow to marinate in the refrigerator for at least 30 minutes. Mix the mayonnaise, horseradish sauce and seasoning together and stir into the salad mixture just before serving. Garnish with the chopped parsley.

CELERIAC WITH CHIVE MAYONNAISE

Serves 4–6

METRIC/IMPERIAL

2 medium celeriac
2 teaspoons lemon juice
chive mayonnaise (see opposite)

Peel the celeriac and shred on a coarse grater. Toss in the lemon juice to prevent discoloration. Combine with the mayonnaise and chill before serving.

MUSHROOMS WITH CHIVE MAYONNAISE

Serves 8

METRIC/IMPERIAL

Chive Mayonnaise

1 tablespoon tomato purée
2 tablespoons Worcestershire sauce
1 teaspoon lemon juice
2 tablespoons chopped chives
2 tablespoons soured cream
300 ml/½ pint thick mayonnaise (see page 180)
seasoning

450 g/1 lb button mushrooms, thinly sliced
8 lettuce leaves

To garnish

8 stuffed green olives
8 wedges of lemon

Combine all the ingredients for the mayonnaise. Keep the sliced mushrooms and mayonnaise in the refrigerator. Fold the mushrooms into the mayonnaise and pile each serving on to a lettuce leaf. Garnish with the stuffed olives and lemon wedges.

MIDDLE EAST VEGETABLE SALAD

Serves 6

METRIC/IMPERIAL

225 g/8 oz crushed wheat
2 tablespoons chopped parsley
1 teaspoon chopped mint
150 g/5 oz spring onions, finely chopped
100 g/4 oz shallots, finely chopped
450 g/1 lb tomatoes, peeled and each cut into eighths
2 teaspoons salt
freshly ground pepper
3 tablespoons lemon juice
5 tablespoons olive oil

Soak the crushed wheat in water for 20–30 minutes before preparing the salad. Drain. Add the vegetables one at a time, mixing thoroughly. Finally add seasoning to taste and the lemon juice and oil.

SPANISH SALAD

Serves 4

METRIC/IMPERIAL

1 large Spanish onion, very thinly sliced
½ cucumber, finely sliced
6 tomatoes, peeled and sliced
2 tablespoons grated Parmesan cheese
seasoning
French dressing (see page 181)
Spanish olives to garnish

Layer all the prepared vegetables in a serving dish, sprinkling a little Parmesan cheese and seasoning between each layer.

Pour over the French dressing just to cover. Garnish with Spanish olives.

INDIAN SALAD

Cooking time 12–15 minutes Serves 4–6

METRIC/IMPERIAL

225 g/8 oz green beans
225 g/8 oz button mushrooms
bunch spring onions
2 teaspoons curry powder
1 (142-ml/5 fl oz) carton soured cream
1 tablespoon lemon juice
2 tablespoons mayonnaise (see page 180)
seasoning
2–3 hard-boiled eggs
2–3 tomatoes, peeled
chopped chives to garnish

Slightly undercook the sliced beans, until tender but still firm. Drain and cool them. Slice the mushrooms and spring onions. Mix together the curry powder, soured cream, lemon juice, mayonnaise and seasoning. Toss the beans, mushrooms and onions in the sauce. Chill for 30 minutes. Serve in a shallow dish, bordered with alternate slices of hard-boiled egg and tomatoes. Sprinkle the top with chopped chives before serving.

Snacks and Savouries

Where do you put all those interesting recipes and ideas that don't fall logically into any of the usual categories? The answer is here. They can be served at virtually any time of day and will be popular with the family as well as with guests.

CHEESE-ONION BALL CANAPÉS

Makes about 16

METRIC/IMPERIAL

100 g/4 oz Cheddar cheese, grated
2 tablespoons grated onion
2 tablespoons (approx) thick soured cream
chopped parsley or chopped nuts

Mix the cheese and onion together, combine with enough soured cream to bind and form into small ball shapes. Roll in chopped parsley or chopped nuts and chill well before serving.

CHICKEN AND EGG BALLS

Serves 4

METRIC/IMPERIAL

225 g/8 oz cooked chicken
6 hard-boiled eggs, finely chopped
1 tablespoon chives
mayonnaise (see page 180)
chopped walnuts

To garnish
sliced tomato
sprigs of parsley

Mince or finely chop the chicken and mix with the eggs and chives. Bind together with the mayonnaise. Divide the mixture into small portions and roll into balls. Roll each ball lightly in the chopped walnuts. Chill until firm and serve with the sliced tomatoes and parsley.

ONION-CHEESE PINWHEEL CANAPÉS

Cooking time 12–15 minutes Makes about 48
Oven temperature Hot 230°C, 450°F, Gas Mark 8

METRIC/IMPERIAL

225 g/8 oz shortcrust pastry (see page 156)
50 g/2 oz cheese, grated
1 onion, finely chopped
seasoning

Roll out the pastry very thinly. Sprinkle on the cheese, onion and seasoning. Roll up like a swiss roll. Wrap tightly in foil or cling film and chill until firm. Cut off in 1-cm/½-inch pieces, securing with a wooden cocktail stick if necessary, and bake cut side uppermost on a baking tray in a hot oven.

CHEESE AND ONION STICKS

Cooking time 15–18 minutes Makes about 100
Oven temperature Hot 220°C, 425°F, Gas Mark 7

METRIC/IMPERIAL

1 onion, grated or finely chopped
100 g/4 oz mature Cheddar cheese, grated
seasoning
1 tablespoon Worcestershire sauce
1 (369-g/13-oz) packet frozen puff pastry, thawed
beaten egg for glazing

Combine the onion, cheese, seasoning and Worcestershire sauce. Roll out the pastry very thinly to a 30 × 35-cm/12 × 14-inch rectangle. Cut this lengthways into four equal strips. Spread the filling on to two of the strips and cover with the other two strips of pastry. Press firmly together and glaze with the beaten egg. Cut into ½-cm/¼-inch wide strips 7.5-cm/3-inch long and bake on a baking sheet until they are risen and golden brown.

GARLIC BREAD STRIPS

Brush thin slices of rye bread with 100 g/4 oz melted butter, to which a clove of crushed garlic has been added. Cut into thin strips, place on a baking sheet and bake in a moderately hot oven, 200°C, 400°F, Gas Mark 6, until lightly browned – about 5 minutes. Serve with savoury dips.

GARLIC CROÛTONS

Remove the crust from a thickly sliced white loaf. Mix 100 g/4 oz butter with ½ clove of garlic, crushed. Spread this onto the slices of bread. Cut into small cubes and either fry, or bake in a hot oven, 230°C, 450°F, Gas Mark 8 for about 8 minutes, until browned.

SAVOURY BUTTERS

Use with hot steaks or chops etc., or piped for canapés, or to make a more interesting flavour for sandwiches.

CHIVE BUTTER

METRIC/IMPERIAL

50 g/2 oz butter
1 tablespoon chopped chives
1 teaspoon lemon juice

GARLIC BUTTER

METRIC/IMPERIAL

50 g/2 oz butter
1 clove garlic, crushed

ONION BUTTER

METRIC/IMPERIAL

50 g/2 oz butter
1 teaspoon onion juice (made from crushed, finely chopped onion)

Cream the butter until light and fluffy and mix in the other ingredients. Store in an air-tight plastic container in the refrigerator, or form into a sausage shape and wrap in foil and refrigerate so that slices may be cut from it.

CHIVE BUTTER

METRIC/IMPERIAL

100 g/4 oz butter, softened
4 tablespoons finely chopped chives
seasoning, lemon juice (optional)

Add the chives when the butter is well softened by whipping (rather than melting), mix thoroughly, adding seasoning and a little lemon juice if desired. Roll into a sausage shape in dampened greaseproof paper or foil and refrigerate until firm. Use by cutting slices of the roll as required for steak, fish, chops, etc.

BUTTER BERCY

Serves 4

METRIC/IMPERIAL

1 small shallot, chopped
4 tablespoons white wine
75 g/3 oz butter, creamed
2 teaspoons chopped parsley
½ teaspoon lemon juice
75–100 g/3–4 oz cooked marrow (from a beef marrow bone)

Simmer the chopped shallot in the wine for about 10 minutes, until the wine has reduced to about 1 tablespoon. Cream the butter and gradually blend in all the other ingredients. Serve with grilled meat or fish.

ONION AND CHEESE SPREAD

Liquidize equal quantities of Gruyère cheese and Spanish onions in a blender. Use as a canapé spread on rye bread.

HAM AND ONION SPREAD

METRIC/IMPERIAL

150 g/5 oz cooked ham, chopped
1 onion, chopped
1 tablespoon sour cream
1 tablespoon mayonnaise
freshly ground black pepper

Liquidize the ingredients in a blender and pipe onto buttered toast shapes.

SPRING ONION AND BUTTER

Cream 100 g/4 oz butter until it is light and fluffy and add a bunch of finely chopped spring onions. Use to fill celery 'boats'.

ONION AND EGG SPREAD

METRIC/IMPERIAL

1 medium onion, finely chopped
1 hard-boiled egg, finely chopped
seasoning
75 g/3 oz softened butter

Combine all the ingredients and serve on rye or pumpernickel bread or crackers.

PÂTÉ DIP

Serves 8

METRIC/IMPERIAL

1 (113-g/4-oz) can liver pâté
1 tablespoon Worcestershire sauce
5 tablespoons double cream, lightly whipped
2 teaspoons chopped chives
1 teaspoon chutney, chopped
1 clove garlic, crushed
seasoning

Carefully mix all the above ingredients together. Place in a covered container in the refrigerator for at least 2 hours, to allow the flavour to mature. Serve with potato crisps, savoury biscuits, or pieces of celery or chicory for dipping.

GARLIC AND COTTAGE CHEESE DIP

Serves 4

METRIC/IMPERIAL

225 g/8 oz cottage cheese
4 tablespoons milk
2 cloves garlic, crushed
salt

Combine all the ingredients and then sieve or liquidize in a blender.
Particularly good served with slices of celery to dip with.

BLENDER GARLIC DIP

Serves 4

METRIC/IMPERIAL

4½ tablespoons milk
2 teaspoons Worcestershire sauce
1 teaspoon paprika
½ clove garlic
1 teaspoon vinegar
225 g/8 oz cream cheese

Blend the milk, Worcestershire sauce, paprika, garlic and vinegar for 10 seconds. Add the cream cheese, a little at a time, with the blender still running. Blend until smooth.

An ideal topping for steak or jacket potatoes, as well as a dip.

PARTY ONIONS

Cooking time 55 minutes Serves 6
Oven temperature Moderate 190°C, 375°F, Gas Mark 5

METRIC/IMPERIAL

500 g/18 oz small onions
250 ml/8 fl oz water
1 tablespoon brown sugar
1 teaspoon salt
½ teaspoon paprika
freshly ground pepper
2 tablespoons chopped almonds
50 g/2 oz butter
25 g/1 oz flour
1 teaspoon Worcestershire sauce

Pour boiling water onto the onions. Allow to stand for a few minutes, drain and peel. Place the water, sugar, salt, paprika and pepper to taste in a saucepan and bring to the boil. Add the onions and boil for 30 minutes. Drain and save the liquid. Place the onions in a greased 1-litre/1¾-pint casserole. Brown the almonds in the butter, add the flour and brown lightly. Stir in the liquid saved from cooking the onions and cook until slightly thickened. Add the Worcestershire sauce and pour over the onions. Cover and bake in a moderate oven for 25 minutes.

ONIONS IN CREAM

Cut large sweet onions into thin slices. Arrange in a baking dish and sprinkle with salt and freshly milled black pepper. Pour over cream to cover. Bake in a moderate oven, 160°C, 325°F, Gas Mark 3 until tender.

SCALLOPED ONIONS

Cover 225 g/8 oz of cooked, thickly sliced onions with 300 ml/½ pint of white sauce (see page 173) in a buttered ovenproof dish. Sprinkle over the top crushed cream cracker crumbs and a little grated cheese, mixed together. Bake in a moderately hot oven, 200°C, 400°F, Gas Mark 6 until brown and crusty.

SPRING ONION TOPS SAVOURY

A way of using up the green tops to spring onions, which are sometimes wasted.

Cover with cold water and cook for 30 minutes. Drain well, then fry in butter, well seasoned with freshly ground black pepper and toss until beginning to turn brown. Serve piled onto buttered toast, as a savoury or starter.

GARLIC OLIVES

Drain a jar of green or black olives into a bowl. Add 6–12 cloves of garlic (to taste), peeled. Cover with salad oil and refrigerate in a sealed container for 24 hours. Drain the oil and use it for making salad dressing. Serve the flavoured olives as hors-d'oeuvres, garnished with chopped parsley.

MARINATED ONIONS

Skin and slice 2–3 large Spanish onions and soak in a brine of 300 ml/½ pint water and 1 tablespoon of salt for several hours. Drain and soak in vinegar for 20–30 minutes. Drain again and chill thoroughly before serving as hors-d'oeuvres.

ICED ONION RINGS

Cut large Spanish onions into thin slices, then press out into rings. Place these in iced water for an hour or two, before draining and drying well and serving on salads.

CURRIED ONION OMELETTE

Cooking time 5 minutes Serves 1

METRIC/IMPERIAL

Filling

1 onion, finely chopped
¼ teaspoon curry powder
1 tablespoon Béchamel sauce (see page 174)

Omelette

3 eggs
3 teaspoons water
seasoning
15 g/½ oz butter

Fry the onion with the curry powder until golden brown and combine with the sauce. Keep warm, ready for filling the omelette.

To make the omelette, beat the eggs, water and seasoning together until well mixed. Heat the butter in a heavy-based pan and just before it turns brown add the egg mixture.

As the egg sets, move it to the centre with a spatula, letting more egg mixture hit the hot base of the pan. When no liquid egg is left, but it is still quite moist, put the filling on the side away from the handle of the pan. Fold over the other side and seal for a moment over the heat. Tip out onto a plate and serve at once.

CHEESE SOUFFLÉ WITH GARLIC CROÛTONS

Cooking time 40–45 minutes Serves 4
Oven temperature Moderately hot 200°C, 400°F, Gas Mark 6

METRIC/IMPERIAL

300 ml/½ pint Béchamel sauce (see page 174)
150 g/5 oz Cheddar cheese, grated
seasoning
½ teaspoon made mustard
6 eggs, separated
4 tablespoons garlic croûtons

Gradually bring the Béchamel sauce to the boil and add the grated cheese, seasoning and mustard. Cook gently until the cheese has completely melted. Remove from the heat and add the egg yolks one at a time. Whisk the egg whites until just stiff. Fold the egg whites and croûtons carefully into the cheese sauce. Pile into a buttered 1-litre/1¾-pint soufflé dish and bake in a moderately hot oven until golden and well risen. Eat immediately.

LEEKS AU GRATIN

Cooking time 45–50 minutes Serves 2
Oven temperature Moderate 180°C, 350°F, Gas Mark 4

METRIC/IMPERIAL

3 leeks
3 rashers bacon, grilled
3 tomatoes, peeled and sliced

Sauce
40 g/1½ oz margarine
40 g/1½ oz plain flour
300 ml/½ pint milk
150 ml/¼ pint leek liquor
75 g/3 oz cheese, grated
seasoning

Topping
1 tablespoon grated cheese
1 tablespoon white breadcrumbs
sliced tomatoes and parsley to garnish

Trim and wash the leeks. Use the green part as well as the white and cook in boiling salted water until tender, 15–20 minutes. Remove the bacon rinds and cut the bacon into small pieces. Drain leeks, cut up coarsely and put into a greased shallow dish. Add the bacon and tomatoes.

Cover with the sauce (see Béchamel sauce for method, page 174). Sprinkle the top with the cheese and breadcrumbs. Reheat in the oven for 20–30 minutes, or brown under the grill. Garnish with sliced tomatoes and parsley.

ONION AND WALNUT LOAF

Cooking time 1 hour Serves 4–6
Oven temperature Moderate 160–180°C, 325–350°F, Gas Mark 3–4

METRIC/IMPERIAL

450 g/1 lb carrots, peeled and sliced into about 1-cm/½-inch pieces
2 large onions, peeled and chopped
50 g/2 oz butter or margarine
100 g/4 oz walnuts, coarsely chopped
175 g/6 oz fresh white breadcrumbs
3 eggs
300 ml/½ pint milk
seasoning

Cook the carrots in boiling salted water for about 5 minutes. Sauté the onions in the butter and add with all the other ingredients to the strained carrots.

Grease a 1 kg/2-lb loaf tin and spoon in the mixture. Cover with foil and bake in a moderate oven for 1 hour. Cool for 5 minutes before turning out.

Serve hot with Italian tomato sauce (see page 177), or cold sliced with cream cheese or butter spread.

POTATO BAKE

Cooking time about 45 minutes Serves 4
Oven temperature Moderate 180°C, 350°F, Gas Mark 4

METRIC/IMPERIAL

1 kg/2 lb potatoes
2 large onions
25 g/1 oz butter
225 g/8 oz Cheddar cheese, grated
chopped parsley
3 eggs
300 ml/½ pint milk
seasoning

Wash the potatoes and boil them whole in their skins. Cool slightly, then peel and dice. Peel and chop the onions and cook in the butter until they are soft and transparent. Mix the potatoes, onions, cheese and parsley together and spread in an ovenproof dish. Beat the eggs, stir in the milk and seasoning and pour over the potato mixture. Bake in a moderate oven for 30 minutes.

Serve with a crisp green salad.

ONION AND POTATO RING

Cooking time 1 hour Serves 4–6
Oven temperature Moderately hot 190°C, 375°F, Gas Mark 5

METRIC/IMPERIAL

500 g/18 oz old potatoes, peeled and grated
350 g/12 oz onions, peeled and grated
50 g/2 oz butter or margarine
175 g/6 oz cheese, coarsely grated
seasoning
½ teaspoon paprika
chopped parsley to garnish

Melt the butter and toss the onions and potatoes with half of the cheese, seasoning well and adding the paprika.

Grease an ovenproof ring mould thoroughly, pile in the mixture and pack down well. Cover with a piece of greased foil. Bake in a moderately hot oven for 45 minutes. Turn out carefully on to an ovenproof plate and spoon over the remaining cheese. Return to the oven for 10–15 minutes for the cheese to melt and brown. Garnish with chopped parsley.

ONION CHEESE SQUARES

Cooking time 1 hour Serves 6–8
Oven temperature Moderate 160°C, 325°F, Gas Mark 3

METRIC/IMPERIAL

3 large onions, sliced
75 g/3 oz butter
4 eggs
900 ml/1½ pints scalded milk
1 teaspoon salt
½ teaspoon celery salt
¼ teaspoon paprika
150 g/5 oz Cheddar cheese, grated
50 g/2 oz red pepper, sliced
150 g/5 oz breadcrumbs
25 g/1 oz chopped parsley

Sauté the onions gently in the butter until soft. Lightly beat the eggs and gradually add the warmed milk, stirring all the time. Combine all the ingredients together and place in a buttered baking dish, 15 × 25 × 5 cm/6 × 10 × 2 inches, and bake in a moderate oven, with the baking dish standing in a tray of hot water, for about an hour. Cut into squares to serve, garnished with slices of stuffed olives, if liked.

SHRIMP TURNOVERS

Cooking time 5 minutes (for frying) Serves 4

METRIC/IMPERIAL

225 g/8 oz peeled shrimps
2 onions, finely chopped
2 tablespoons oil
3 eggs, separated
25 g/1 oz flour
1 tablespoon chopped chives
seasoning
450 g/1 lb shortcrust pastry (see page 156)
oil for deep frying

Brown the shrimps and onions in the oil. Remove from the heat and add the egg yolks, flour, chives and seasoning. Beat the egg whites until stiff and fold into the shrimp mixture.

Roll out the pastry very thinly and cut into rounds, 10 cm/4 inches in diameter. Place a good tablespoon of shrimp mixture on each pastry round. Moisten the edges of the pastry and fold over to seal. Deep fry in oil until golden brown, about 5 minutes. Drain on absorbent paper and serve at once.

FISH PATTIES

Cooking time 15–20 minutes Serves 4–6

METRIC/IMPERIAL

6 tablespoons chopped onion
2 tablespoons melted butter
4 tablespoons lemon juice
8 tablespoons fresh white breadcrumbs
2 eggs, beaten
3 tablespoons chopped parsley
1 teaspoon dry mustard
1 (198-g/7-oz) can pink salmon or tuna, drained
3 tablespoons melted butter

Cook the onions in 2 tablespoons butter until soft. Add the lemon juice, half the crumbs, the eggs, parsley, mustard and fish; mix well.

Shape into even-sized patties and roll each in the remaining crumbs. Fry the coated patties in the remaining butter over a medium heat, until browned on both sides.

Serve with tartare sauce (see page 180).

QUICK ONION KÜCHEN

Cooking time 25 minutes Serves 4
Oven temperature Moderate 190°C, 375°F, Gas Mark 5

METRIC/IMPERIAL

4 large onions, sliced
25 g/1 oz butter
2 eggs, beaten
250 ml/8 fl oz soured cream
½ teaspoon salt
freshly ground pepper
4 slices rye bread
4 rashers streaky bacon, halved

Sauté the onions in the butter until they are tender. Mix the eggs, soured cream and seasoning, to taste. Place the bread in a shallow greased dish and cover with the onions. Pour the egg mixture over and top with the bacon. Bake in a moderate oven, uncovered, until the bacon is crisp – about 25 minutes.

HAMBURGER PIE

Cooking time 20–25 minutes Serves 2
Oven temperature Hot 220°C, 425°F, Gas Mark 7

METRIC/IMPERIAL

1 (250-g/7½-oz) packet puff pastry
4 beefburgers
¼ white cabbage, finely chopped
1 clove garlic, crushed (optional)
50 g/2 oz Cheddar cheese, grated
seasoning
beaten egg or milk for glazing

Line an 18-cm/7 inch flan ring with two-thirds of the pastry, leaving a 1-cm/½-inch overhang. Place the beefburgers in the flan case and cover with a mixture of the cabbage, garlic, cheese and seasoning. Roll out the remaining pastry to an 18-cm/7-inch circle for the lid, dampen the edges of the overhang, place the lid on top and seal well. Flute edges. Make 6 radial slits from the centre of the lid.

Brush round the centre with egg or milk and fold back from the centre to make an opening in the centre of the pie. Brush the pie with egg or milk. Bake in a hot oven, removing flan ring after 15 minutes.

CRACKER CHEESE FLAN

Cooking time 40–45 minutes Serves 4–6
Oven temperature Moderate 160°C, 325°F, Gas Mark 3

METRIC/IMPERIAL

About 33 cream crackers, crushed
100 g/4 oz butter or margarine, melted
3 onions, thinly sliced
25 g/1 oz butter or margaine
450 ml/¾ pint milk
3 eggs, beaten
1 teaspoon salt
¼ teaspoon black pepper
225 g/8 oz Cheddar cheese, finely grated

Combine the cracker crumbs and melted butter. Mix thoroughly and press evenly into a buttered deep 23-cm/9-inch flan dish.

Fry the onions in the 25 g/1 oz butter until they are lightly browned and place them in the cracker case. Scald the milk, beat in the eggs, seasoning and cheese and pour over the onions. Bake in a moderate oven. Serve hot or cold from the dish.

SPRING ONION AND CRESS QUICHE

Cooking time 25 minutes Serves 4–6
Oven temperature Moderately hot 190°C, 375°F, Gas Mark 5

METRIC/IMPERIAL

175 g/6 oz wholewheat pastry (see page 154)
14 spring onions, finely chopped
1 bunch watercress, finely chopped
15 g/½ oz butter
3 large eggs
150 ml/¼ pint single cream
seasoning
100 g/4 oz Cheddar cheese, grated

Line a 20-cm/8-inch flan ring or dish with the pastry and bake blind.

Fry the onions and watercress gently in the butter for about 5 minutes. Beat the eggs and add the single cream with the seasoning and half of the grated cheese. Place the onion mixture in the base of the pastry case, pour over the egg mixture and top with the remaining grated cheese.

Bake until the custard is set and browned. Serve hot or cold.

ONION TART

Cooking time 45 minutes Serves 4
Oven temperature Moderately hot 200°C, 400°F, Gas Mark 6 – 10 minutes Moderate 180°C, 350°F, Gas Mark 4 – 35 minutes

METRIC/IMPERIAL

350 g/12 oz shortcrust pastry (see page 156)
450 g/1 lb onions, sliced
25 g/1 oz butter
25 g/1 oz flour
75 ml/4 tablespoons single cream
2 eggs
seasoning
150 ml/¼ pint milk

Topping
25 g/1 oz fresh breadcrumbs
25 g/1 oz cheese, grated

Line a flan dish or flan ring with the pastry and bake blind in a moderately hot oven for 10 minutes. Sauté the onions in the butter until they are soft but not browned. Stir in the flour and put the mixture into the base of the flan case. Lightly whip the cream and eggs together with seasoning, combine with the milk and pour over the onions. Mix the breadcrumbs and cheese together, sprinkle on top and bake in a moderate oven until the topping is crusty and golden, about 35 minutes.

LEEK AND BACON TARTLETS

Cooking time 25–35 minutes Serves 8 (as a starter)
Oven temperature Moderate 180°C, 350°F, Gas Mark 4

METRIC/IMPERIAL

225 g/8 oz shortcrust pastry (see page 156)
50 g/2 oz margarine
175 g/6 oz bacon, diced
2 large leeks, finely sliced
300 ml/½ pint milk
40 g/1½ oz flour
1 onion stock cube
150 ml/¼ pint single cream
2 teaspoons chopped parsley
75 g/3 oz cheese, grated

To garnish
8 bacon rolls
sprigs of parsley

Bake the tartlet cases blind in the middle of a moderate oven. For the filling, sauté the diced bacon and leeks in the margarine until soft. Make up the sauce (one-stage, see page 173) by whisking the milk, flour, margarine and crumbled onion cube together, until it is thickened and smooth. Cook for about 2 minutes before adding the cream, chopped parsley, and bacon and leek mixture. Divide the mixture between the tartlet cases and sprinkle each with a little grated cheese. Either brown in a moderate oven for 10–15 minutes or under the grill. Serve hot, garnished with cooked bacon rolls and sprigs of parsley.

ONION, BACON AND APPLE PIE

Cooking time 1¼ hours Serves 4
Oven temperature Moderate 180°C, 350°F, Gas Mark 4

METRIC/IMPERIAL

225 g/8 oz bacon
450 g/1 lb onions, sliced
seasoning
2 teaspoons dried sage
450 g/1 lb cooking apples, peeled, cored and sliced
1 tablespoon castor sugar
250 ml/8 fl oz water
225 g/8 oz shortcrust pastry (see page 156)

Remove the rind from the bacon and use to line a pie dish. Place the onions on top and season with salt, pepper and half the sage. Cover with the apples, more seasoning, the remaining sage and the sugar. Add the water and cover the pie dish with the pastry. Bake in a moderate oven until golden brown.

COUNTRY GARDEN FLAN

Cooking time 30–35 minutes Serves 4
Oven temperature Moderately hot 200°C, 400°F, Gas Mark 6

METRIC/IMPERIAL

Pastry
100 g/4 oz plain flour
100 g/4 oz wheatmeal flour
pinch salt
50 g/2 oz butter or margarine
50 g/2 oz lard
2 tablespoons water

Filling
1 tablespoon oil
1 large onion, sliced
2 tablespoons Worcestershire sauce
2 medium carrots, peeled
100 g/4 oz cut green beans, fresh or frozen
1 tomato, peeled and sliced
100 g/4 oz Cheddar cheese, grated
seasoning
2 eggs, beaten
150 ml/¼ pint milk

Combine the flours and salt in a bowl. Rub in the fats until the mixture resembles fine breadcrumbs, add the water and mix to a firm dough. Turn out onto a lightly floured surface and knead until smooth. Roll out and line a 20-cm/8-inch flan ring or a shallow pie dish, then chill the pastry. Heat the oil in a pan, add the onion and fry until soft, about 5 minutes. Add the Worcestershire sauce, fry for a further 2 minutes and allow to cool. Cook the carrots in boiling salted water for 5 minutes, add the beans and cook for a further 5 minutes, then drain well.

Spread the onion over the base of the pastry case and layer with the carrots, beans, tomato and cheese, seasoning between each layer. Beat together the eggs and milk and pour into the flan case. Bake in a moderately hot oven for 30–35 minutes, until the filling has set and the pastry is crisp and golden brown.

Baking

I am indebted to the home economists at the Flour Advisory Bureau for coming up with some excellent *new* recipes, in response to my challenge to them about incorporating onions into breads, pastries, scones, etc. The results of their experiments are excitingly different, as you too will find when you try them.

They commented that chives lose flavour in the drier mixtures, but give a delicate flavour to breads, scones, suetcrust pastry, flaky pastry and tea-breads.

Garlic salt is a satisfactory alternative to garlic, where relatively large amounts of salt are required, e.g. in bread, or where only a mild flavour is preferable.

Onion must be chopped *very* finely for pastry as the size of the pieces determines the thickness to which the pastry may be rolled; grating the onion is usually preferable.

SHORTCRUST PASTRY

Cooking time see separate recipes

METRIC/IMPERIAL

225 g/8 oz white or brown plain flour
good pinch salt
50 g/2 oz margarine or butter
50 g/2 oz cooking fat
about 2 tablespoons cold water

Mix together the flour and salt. Rub in the margarine or butter, and fat until the mixture resembles fine breadcrumbs. Mix in enough cold water to make a firm dough. Turn on to a lightly floured surface and knead lightly until smooth. Roll out and use as required.

Variations

Onion Pastry:
Grate one small onion and stir into the rubbed-in mixture. Continue as above.

Garlic Pastry:
Crush 2 cloves garlic and work to a paste with ½ teaspoon salt. Blend with cold water and continue as above.

Cheese shortcrust:
Add 75 g/3 oz finely grated cheese to the rubbed-in fat and flour, together with pinch of cayenne pepper; continue as above.

Cheese and Onion Twirls:
Roll out the Onion Pastry to a 30-cm/12-inch square. Brush with beaten egg and sprinkle 175 g/6 oz finely grated cheese on top. Cut the pastry into 9 squares. Roll up each piece Swiss roll fashion, place on a greased baking tray. Brush again with beaten egg, sprinkle with poppy seeds. Bake in a moderately hot oven 200°C, 400°F, Gas Mark 6 for 15–20 minutes, until crisp and golden brown.

BASIC FLAKY PASTRY RECIPE

Cooking time see separate recipes

METRIC/IMPERIAL

225 g/8 oz plain white flour
½ teaspoon salt
175 g/6 oz hard margarine and lard blended together and chilled
2 teaspoons lemon juice
about 150 ml/¼ pint cold water

Sift together the flour and salt. Rub in a quarter of the fat. Stir in the lemon juice and enough water to make a pliable dough. Divide the remaining fat into three equal portions.

First rolling: Roll the dough to an oblong 45 × 15 cm/18 × 6 inches, keeping the edges straight. Dot one portion of fat in small pieces over the top two-thirds of the dough, leaving a 1-cm/½-in border along the top and sides. Fold uncovered bottom third up and the top third down and over it. Turn the dough so the folded edge is on the left-hand side. Seal the edges by pressing with a rolling pin.

Second rolling: Roll the dough to an oblong 45 × 15 cm/18 × 6 inches. Add the second portion of fat and fold as before. Cover and chill for 15 minutes.

Third rolling: As for second rolling, using the last portion of fat. There is no need to chill the dough.

Fourth rolling: As for second rolling, without adding any fat. Cover and chill for 15 minutes.

Use as required.

Variation

Flaky Pastry with Chives
Before the first rolling of the dough, sprinkle a tablespoon of chopped chives over the fat. Fold, seal and turn the pastry as before. Add a further 2 tablespoons of chopped chives with the second and third rollings.

BASIC CHOUX PASTRY RECIPE

Cooking time see individual recipes

METRIC/IMPERIAL

65 g/2½ oz plain flour
pinch salt
50 g/2 oz butter or margarine
150 ml/¼ pint water
2 eggs

Sift together the flour and salt. Melt the fat in the water and bring to the boil. Remove from the heat and stir in the flour. Beat until the paste is smooth and forms a ball in the pan. Cool slightly. Beat the eggs and add a little at a time to the paste, beating well between each addition. The mixture should be smooth and glossy and of piping consistency. Use as required.

Variations

Choux pastry with garlic:
Replace the salt in the basic recipe with garlic salt and beat one clove of garlic, worked to a paste, into the mixture.

Choux pastry with onion:
Finely chop one medium onion and beat into the mixture.

SUET CRUST PASTRY

Cooking time see separate recipes

METRIC/IMPERIAL

225 g/8 oz self-raising flour
1 teaspoon salt
100 g/4 oz shredded suet
150 ml/¼ pint water

Sift together the flour and salt, stir in the suet. Using a round bladed knife, mix with enough water to make a soft dough. Knead lightly. Use as required.

Variations

Sage and Onion Suet Crust Pastry:
Finely chop 1 medium onion and 1 tablespoon fresh sage; stir into the dry ingredients. Continue as above.

Suet Crust Pastry with Chives:
Stir 2 tablespoons chopped fresh chives into the dry ingredients. Continue as above.

SCONES

Cooking time 8–10 minutes Makes approximately 8
Oven temperature Hot 220–230°C, 425–450°F, Gas Mark 7–8

METRIC/IMPERIAL

225 g/8 oz self-raising flour	generous pinch salt
Or 225 g/8 oz plain flour + 3 teaspoons baking powder	50 g/2 oz butter or margarine
	150 ml/¼ pint milk

Sieve the flour with the other dry ingredients. Rub in the fat until the mixture resembles fine breadcrumbs. Add the milk to the dry ingredients and mix to a soft dough. Roll out lightly on a floured board to about 1.5 cm/¾ inch thickness. Cut into rounds, using a 6-cm/2½-inch cutter. Put on to a baking tray and bake for about 10 minutes towards the top of a hot oven, until golden brown.

Variations

Onion Scones:
Finely chop one medium onion and stir into the rubbed-in mixture. Continue as above.

Cheese and Garlic Scones:
Stir 50 g/2 oz grated cheese into the rubbed in mixture. Crush 1 clove garlic and work to a paste with ½ teaspoon salt. Blend with the milk and continue as above.

Scones with Chives:
Stir 3 tablespoons chopped chives into the rubbed-in mixture. Continue as above.

Scones with Spring Onions:
Stir 4 tablespoons chopped spring onions into the rubbed-in mixture. Continue as above.

PISSALADIÈRE

Cooking time 30–35 minutes Serves 4–6
Oven temperature Moderately hot 190°C, 375°F, Gas Mark 5

METRIC/IMPERIAL

175 g/6 oz shortcrust pastry (see page 156)
1 (50-g/2-oz) can anchovy fillets
little milk
1 large green pepper, seeded and thinly sliced
1 large onion, thinly sliced
25 g/1 oz butter
1 (397-g/14-oz) can tomatoes
1½ teaspoons sugar
½ teaspoon each of marjoram, basil and oregano *or* 1½ teaspoons dried mixed herbs
seasoning
Parmesan cheese

Line a 20-cm/8-inch flan ring or dish with the pastry and bake blind for 10–15 minutes. Put the anchovy fillets in a saucer of milk and leave for 15 minutes, then drain.

Fry the green pepper and onion in the butter, until golden brown. Add the tomatoes, sugar, herbs and seasoning and cook for a further 10–15 minutes.

Place the mixture in the pastry case and make a lattice top with the anchovy fillets; sprinkle with the grated Parmesan cheese. Bake for about 20 minutes.

Variation
This filling mixture is good on a traditional Pizza base (see page 170).

COTTAGE CHEESE D'ARTOIS

Cooking time 15–20 minutes Serves 4
Oven temperature Hot 230°C, 450°F, Gas Mark 8

METRIC/IMPERIAL

Flaky Pastry made with 100 g /4 oz flour, etc. (see page 157)

Filling
25 g/1 oz butter
1 medium onion
1 egg
50 g/2 oz Cheddar cheese
1 (113-g/4-oz) carton cottage cheese
seasoning

First prepare the flaky pastry. Peel and roughly chop the onion. Melt the butter in a small saucepan, add the onion and cook gently until the onion is soft but not browned. Place the egg in a liquidiser goblet. Cut the Cheddar into 1-cm/½-inch cubes and add to the liquidiser with the cottage cheese, onion and butter; season well. Run the machine until the mixture is evenly blended. Roll out the pastry on a floured board to a 30-cm/12-inch square. Trim the edges and place on a dampened baking tray. Pour the cottage cheese mixture onto one half of the pastry, leaving a 2.5-cm/1-inch border around the edge. Brush the border with beaten egg or milk. Fold over the pastry and seal the edges together firmly. Brush the pastry with beaten egg or milk. Make diagonal cuts along the top of the slice, 5 cm/2 inches apart, through one layer of the pastry. Bake in the centre of a hot oven for 15–20 minutes, until risen and golden brown. Serve warm, cut into slices.

SAVOURY PUFFS

Cooking time 15 minutes Makes 25 Puffs
Oven temperature Moderately hot 200°C, 400°F, Gas Mark 6

METRIC/IMPERIAL

Choux pastry made with 65 g /2½ oz flour, etc. (see page 158)

Filling
100 g/4 oz cream cheese
225 g/8 oz cottage cheese with pineapple
2 tablespoons chopped chives
seasoning

Place teaspoonfuls of choux pastry on greased baking trays and bake in a moderately hot oven until golden brown and crisp. Cool on a wire cooling tray.

To prepare the filling, blend together the cream cheese and cottage cheese, then mix in the chives and season well. Place the mixture in a forcing bag fitted with a 1-cm/½-inch nozzle. Pipe a small amount of filling into each puff.

GOLDEN LAYER PUDDING

Cooking time 1¾ hours Serves 6

METRIC/IMPERIAL

Suet crust pastry with chives, made with 225 g/8 oz self-raising flour, etc. (see page 159)
2 medium onions, peeled and sliced
1 tablespoon oil
225 g/8 oz cheese, grated
seasoning

Roll out the pastry to 1 cm/½ inch thick. Cut into 3 circles of 10 cm/4 inches, 12.5 cm/5 inches and 15 cm/6 inches in diameter. Lightly fry the onions in the oil until soft. Remove from the heat and stir in the cheese. Grease a 1-litre/1¾-pint pudding basin thoroughly with butter. Place the smallest circle of pastry into the basin and cover with half of the cheese and onion mixture. Season well. Repeat layers, finishing with pastry. Cover the basin tightly with foil. Steam for approximately 1¾ hours over boiling water.

DEVILLED KIDNEY GOUGÈRE

Cooking time 50–60 minutes Serves 4
Oven temperature Moderately hot 200°C, 400°F, Gas Mark 6

METRIC/IMPERIAL

Choux pastry made with 65 g/2½ oz flour, etc. (see page 158).

Filling

225 g/8 oz lamb's kidneys
25 g/1 oz butter or margarine
1 large onion, chopped
50 g/2 oz mushrooms, sliced
25 g/1 oz plain flour
2 teaspoons dry mustard
150 ml/¼ pint beef stock
2 teaspoons Worcestershire sauce
chopped chives to garnish

First prepare the choux pastry. Slice the kidneys in half, remove the core and cut into small pieces. Melt the butter in a pan, add the onion and fry gently until softened – about 3 minutes. Add the mushrooms and kidneys and cook for a further 2 minutes. Stir in the flour and dry mustard powder and cook for 1 minute. Gradually blend in the stock and Worcestershire sauce. Bring to the boil, stirring all the time. Reduce the heat and simmer for 10 minutes.

Grease a shallow 23-cm/9-inch ovenproof dish. Spoon choux pastry around the edge of the dish to form a border. Pour the kidney mixture into the centre and bake in the centre of a moderately hot oven for 35–40 minutes until well risen and golden brown. Serve garnished with chopped chives.

AIGRETTES

Cooking time 5 minutes Makes approx 24

METRIC/IMPERIAL

Choux pastry made with 65 g/2½ oz flour, etc. (see page 158)
Oil for deep frying

Have ready a deep frying pan, one-third filled with oil. Heat the oil to 180°C/360°F. Drop teaspoonfuls of the mixture into the fat and fry for 5–6 minutes, until puffed and light golden brown.

When cooked, remove and drain on absorbent kitchen paper. Serve warm.

ONION AND PEPPER KÜCHEN

Cooking time 25–30 minutes
Serves 8
Oven temperature Moderately hot 190°C, 375°F, Gas Mark 5

METRIC/IMPERIAL

Scone dough made with 225g /8 oz flour, etc. (see page 159)

Filling

225 g/8 oz onions, peeled and sliced
1 red pepper, seeded and chopped
25 g/1 oz butter or margarine
15 g/½ oz plain flour
150 ml/¼ pint milk
generous pinch garlic salt
seasoning
1 teaspoon poppy seeds

Roll out the scone dough and line the bases of two 15-cm/6-inch sandwich tins. Fry the onions and pepper in the butter or margarine until tender. Stir in the flour and cook for 1 minute. Add the milk and bring to the boil, stirring. Boil for 1 minute. Stir in the garlic salt and season to taste. Spoon the onion mixture onto the scone base and sprinkle with poppy seeds. Bake for 20 minutes in a moderately hot oven.

GARDENERS' TEA BREAD

Cooking time 50 minutes
Oven temperature Moderately hot 200°C, 400°F, Gas Mark 6

METRIC/IMPERIAL

450 g/1 lb self-raising flour
1 teaspoon salt
50 g/2 oz butter or margarine
6 spring onions, finely chopped
50 g/2 oz walnuts, chopped
2 eggs, beaten
300 ml/½ pint milk

Sift together the flour and salt. Rub in the fat. Stir in the onions and walnuts. Stir in the eggs and milk and mix to a stiff dropping consistency. Spoon into a greased 1-kg/2-lb loaf tin, smooth the top and brush with a little milk to glaze. Bake in a moderately hot oven for 50 minutes, or until golden brown.

Variations

Apple and Chive Bread:
Stir 2 eating apples, peeled, cored and sliced, with 25 g/1 oz soft brown sugar and 3 tablespoons chopped chives into the rubbed-in mixture. Continue as above.

Provençale Loaf:
Stir 3 cloves garlic, crushed, 1 tablespoon mixed herbs, 1 tablespoon chopped parsley and 3 tomatoes, roughly chopped, into the rubbed-in mixture. Continue as above.

BASIC BREAD RECIPE

Cooking time 50 minutes for loaf, 15–20 minutes for rolls
Oven temperature Hot 230°C, 450°F, Gas Mark 8
Makes 1 large loaf or 12 rolls

METRIC/IMPERIAL

Yeast Liquid

2 teaspoons dried yeast + 1 teaspoon sugar *OR* 15g/½ oz fresh yeast
300 ml/½ pint hand-hot water

Other ingredients

450 g/1 lb strong white, brown or wholemeal flour
1½ teaspoons salt
15 g/½ oz lard

Stir the dried yeast and sugar into the water and leave until the yeast has dissolved and the mixture is frothy, about 10 minutes, *OR* blend the fresh yeast with the water and use straight away

Mix together the flour and salt in a large mixing bowl. Rub in the lard. Stir in the yeast liquid and mix to form a dough. Turn the dough onto a lightly floured surface and knead until smooth, elastic and no longer sticky.

To knead: Fold the dough in half towards you, then push down and away from you using the heels of your hands. Give the dough a quarter turn and repeat the folding and pushing action, developing a rocking rhythm. At first the dough may feel soft and sticky, but do not add too much flour at this stage, as it will improve with kneading.

Place the dough inside a large lightly oiled polythene bag, so that the surface of the dough does not dry out, and leave in a warm place until the dough has doubled in size, about 1 hour.

Knock back the risen dough by kneading as before.

Shaping Suggestions:

1. *Tin loaf:* Form the dough into a loaf shape to fit a 1-kg/2-lb greased loaf tin. Dust the top of the loaf with flour.
2. *Bumpy Loaf:* Divide the dough into five equal pieces, shape each piece into a ball, then squash them into oblongs to fit across the width of a 1-kg/2-lb greased loaf tin. Glaze with milk.

3. *Plait:* Divide the dough into three equal pieces. Roll each piece into a sausage shape 40 cm/16 inches long. Join the three strands together at one end. Plait loosely and pinch the ends firmly together. Place on a greased baking sheet. Glaze with beaten egg or milk and sprinkle with poppy seeds or cracked wheat.
4. *Soft sided rolls:* Divide the dough into twelve equal pieces. Roll each piece into a ball, using the palm of the hand. Place close together on a large greased baking sheet, so that they join up on proving. Glaze with beaten egg or milk.

Replace the shaped dough inside the oiled polythene bag and leave to prove until doubled in size – about 45 minutes for a loaf, 25 minutes for rolls. Bake in a hot oven until browned and hollow sounding when tapped on the bottom – about 50 minutes for a loaf, 20 minutes for rolls. Cool on a wire rack.

Variations

Onion, Bacon and Raisin Bread:
Coarsely chop 2 large onions and 100 g/4 oz streaky bacon. Fry gently until the onion is soft and the bacon is cooked. Mix in 50 g/2 oz seedless raisins. Knead this mixture into the risen dough until evenly distributed. Shape, prove and bake dough as above.

Walnut, Cheese and Chive Bread:
Knead 50 g/2 oz chopped walnuts, 100 g/4 oz grated cheese and 2 tablespoons chopped chives into the risen dough until evenly distributed. Shape, prove and bake the dough as above.

Orange, Garlic and Parsley Bread:
Either replace salt in the basic recipe with garlic salt or use 2 cloves garlic, finely chopped. Cut ½ orange into several pieces and liquidise until finely blended. Knead the garlic (if used), orange and 2 tablespoons chopped parsley into the risen dough. Shape, prove and bake the dough as above.

GARLIC BREAD

Cooking time 15 minutes Serves 4
Oven temperature Moderate 180°C, 350°F, Gas Mark 4

METRIC/IMPERIAL

6 cloves garlic, crushed
175 g/6 oz butter
1 French loaf

Beat the crushed garlic into the butter until well blended. Cut into the French loaf at about 3.5-cm/1½-inch intervals, not quite through to the bottom crust. Spread each cut slice liberally with the garlic butter. Wrap the loaf in foil and heat through in a moderate oven until crisp.

FRENCH ONION BREAD

Cooking time 50 minutes Serves 4–6
Oven temperature Moderate 180°C, 350°F, Gas Mark 4

METRIC/IMPERIAL

100 g/4 oz butter
1 (500-ml/1-pint) packet onion soup
1 long French loaf

Soften the butter and add the onion soup mix. Cut the loaf in half lengthways and spread with the butter mixture.

Wrap in foil and freeze. Bake straight from the freezer in a moderate oven for 40 minutes. Open up foil for a further 10 minutes to crisp.

CHEESE AND ONION SMØRHORN

Cooking time 10–15 minutes Makes 16
Oven temperature Hot 230°C, 450°F, Gas Mark 8

METRIC/IMPERIAL

Yeast liquid

1 tablespoon dried yeast + 1 teaspoon sugar *OR* 25 g/1 oz fresh yeast
150 ml/¼ pint hand-hot milk

Other ingredients

100 g/4 oz butter, melted and cooled
1 egg
450 g/1 lb strong white flour
100 g/4 oz cheese, finely grated
1 large onion, finely chopped
1 teaspoon salt
1 teaspoon sugar
beaten egg to glaze

Stir the dried yeast and sugar into the milk and leave until frothy – about 15 minutes, *OR* blend the fresh yeast with the milk.

Beat together the melted butter, egg and yeast liquid. Mix the flour with 75 g/3 oz of the cheese, the onion, salt and sugar. Stir in the yeast liquid and mix to a firm dough. Turn on to a lightly floured surface and knead until the dough is smooth and elastic – about 8 minutes (to knead, see the method for Basic Bread Recipe, page 166). Place the dough inside a large, lightly oiled polythene bag and leave the dough to relax for 5 minutes.

Divide the dough in half and roll each piece into a circle 30 cm/12 inches in diameter. Cut each circle into 8 sections. Brush with egg glaze and roll up each triangle, starting from the widest end. Curve round into a crescent shape and place on a greased baking tray. Glaze with beaten egg and sprinkle the remaining cheese on top. Cover and leave in a warm place until doubled in size – about 1–1½ hours.

Bake in a hot oven for 10–15 minutes, or until golden brown in colour. Cool on a wire rack.

PIZZA

Cooking time 20–30 minutes Serves 6–8
Oven temperature Hot 220°C, 425°F, Gas Mark 7

METRIC/IMPERIAL

1 teaspoon dried yeast plus ¼ teaspoon sugar *OR* 7 g/¼ oz fresh yeast
150 ml/¼ pint warm water
1 teaspoon salt
225 g/8 oz strong plain flour
2 teaspoons oil + 1 teaspoon for brushing top of dough

Grease a loose bottomed 23-cm/9-inch flan tin thoroughly. Stir the dried yeast and sugar in the warm water and leave for about 15 minutes until frothy, or blend fresh yeast with the water. Add the salt to the flour, make a well in the centre and add the yeast mixture and the 2 teaspoons oil. Stir until it comes away from the bowl in one piece of dough.

Knead for about 8–10 minutes on a well-floured surface, then return to the bowl, cover with cling film and leave until its size is doubled. Knock back again on a floured board and then shape into the flan ring.

Brush lightly with oil before covering with one of the following toppings.

Bake in the centre of the oven until the dough is cooked and the topping bubbly and appetising.

Note
Individual pizzas may be made rather than one large one – the cooking time is obviously shorter.

Traditional topping

METRIC/IMPERIAL

1 large onion, finely chopped
25 g/1 oz butter
1 (397-g/14-oz) can tomatoes
½ teaspoon sugar
½ teaspoon chopped or dried basil, marjoram and oregano
seasoning
175 g/6 oz Mozzarella cheese (Cheddar will do)

To garnish
Usually black olives, but green, preferably pimento stuffed, are fine.

Method

Gently fry the onion in the butter until soft but not browned. Add the tomatoes, sugar, herbs and seasoning, and cook until the mixture is well blended and slightly thickened. Slice the cheese (or grate the Cheddar) thinly and place two-thirds on the dough base. Cover with the tomato mixture, arrange the remaining cheese – if sliced in pin-wheel fashion (otherwise sprinkle over grated cheese) and decorate with the olives.

Four flavour topping

1 large onion, finely chopped
25 g/1 oz butter
50 g/2 oz cooked ham, finely diced
½ large green pepper, seeded and thinly sliced
100 g/4 oz mushrooms, thinly sliced
4 tablespoons tomato purée
1 teaspoon sugar
2 teaspoons mixed herbs (dried will do)
1 teaspoon lemon juice
seasoning
3 tablespoons water
100 g/4 oz Mozzarella cheese (Cheddar will do)
1 tablespoon grated Parmesan cheese (optional)

Method

Gently fry the onion in the butter until soft but not browned, remove from the pan. Fry the ham, pepper and mushrooms separately one after the other in the given order.

Mix together the tomato purée, sugar, herbs, lemon juice, seasoning and water.

Cover the pizza base with sliced Mozzarella cheese (or all but 1 tablespoon grated Cheddar), then spread the tomato mixture evenly over the cheese base.

Top with the fried onion, ham, mushrooms, pepper, allowing each ingredient to cover *one quarter* of the pizza. Sprinkle with Parmesan or a tablespoon of grated cheddar and bake as recommended.

Anchovy or Neapolitan topping

METRIC/IMPERIAL

1 (50-g/2-oz) can anchovy fillets
2–3 tablespoons milk
1 large onion, finely chopped
25 g/1 oz butter
1 (397-g/14-oz) can tomatoes
1 teaspoon sugar
½ teaspoon chopped or dried oregano, basil and marjoram
seasoning
100–175 g/4–6 oz Mozzarella or Cheddar cheese
about 10 black olives

Method

Cover the drained anchovies with the milk and leave for at least an hour to remove the saltiness.

Gently fry the onion in the butter until soft but not browned, add the tomatoes, sugar, herbs and seasoning and cook, stirring occasionally, until quite thick (about 15–20 minutes). Cover the pizza dough with the sliced or grated cheese (leaving a little for the top), then spread over the tomato mixture. Drain the anchovies and dab dry with kitchen paper, arrange pin-wheel fashion on top with the black olives between. Sprinkle on the remaining cheese and bake as recommended.

Mock Pizza

Using a scone mixture (see page 159) a very successful pizza-type dish may be made. Roll out the scone mixture to about 5 mm/¼ inch thick and cover with any of the given fillings and bake for the same time and at the same temperature.

Note

Any of the toppings put onto either half a large bready tea-cake (like those in the North of England) or on a pikelet (or crumpet) make delicious snacks.

Sauces, Dressings and Stuffings

Perhaps it is here that the real secret of flavour lies, for the salad without its dressing, the meat or fish without its sauce or gravy are often dull and uninteresting. Few of us can afford the choice cuts of meat and fish which need little or no garnishing, but many cheaper cuts can become worthy of a celebration dinner if accompanied by a carefully chosen and prepared sauce. Vegetables, salads and left-overs too, can be transformed by the judicious use of sauces and dressings.

BASIC WHITE SAUCE, ALL-IN-ONE METHOD

Cooking time about 5 minutes Makes 300 ml/½ pint

METRIC/IMPERIAL

25 g/1 oz margarine or butter
25 g/1 oz plain flour
300 ml/½ pint milk

Place all the ingredients in a saucepan over a moderate heat. Bring to the boil, whisking continually. Cook for 2–3 minutes, still whisking, until thick, smooth and glossy.

Variations

Cheese sauce
Add 50 g/2 oz of well-flavoured grated cheese and a pinch of mustard. Do not allow the sauce to boil after adding the cheese.

Basic Onion sauce
Add 2 boiled and finely chopped onions.

BÉCHAMEL SAUCE

Cooking time 5–10 minutes Makes 500 ml/17 fl oz

METRIC/IMPERIAL

½ onion
1 stalk celery
1 sprig thyme
½ bay leaf
6 peppercorns
500 ml/17 fl oz milk
50 g/2 oz butter
2 tablespoons flour
salt
grated nutmeg

Place the onion, celery, herbs and peppercorns in the milk and bring to the boil. Set aside for 30 minutes. Melt the butter, add the flour and cook for 1 minute. Strain the milk and gradually add to the roux, stirring all the time. Bring to the boil, add the salt and a little grated nutmeg. Simmer for 2–3 minutes and season to taste.

This basic white sauce may be flavoured with cheese, parsley, onion, etc. as required.

ESPAGNOLE SAUCE

Cooking time $1\frac{1}{2}$–2 hours Makes 500 ml/17 fl oz

METRIC/IMPERIAL

50 g/2 oz green streaky bacon
2 carrots
1 Spanish onion
2 stalks celery
2 tablespoons dripping
1 clove garlic, crushed
50 g/2 oz flour
750 ml/$1\frac{1}{4}$ pints beef stock, or water
1 bouquet garni
3 tablespoons tomato purée

Chop the bacon, carrots, onion and celery coarsely. Fry in the dripping with the garlic until golden brown. Add the flour and cook slowly until it is browned, which may take 30 minutes. Add half the stock and stir until the sauce thickens. Add the remaining stock with the bouquet garni and tomato purée and bring to the boil. Simmer very slowly for $1\frac{1}{2}$ hours, stirring frequently. Skim off any fat. Strain through a sieve.

SAUCE BORDELAISE 1

Cooking time 10 minutes Serves 4

METRIC/IMPERIAL

2 shallots, finely chopped
150 ml/$\frac{1}{4}$ pint dry red wine
300 ml/$\frac{1}{2}$ pint Espagnole sauce (see above)
little finely diced beef bone marrow, if possible
parsley, finely chopped

Cook the shallots in the wine until the liquor has reduced by half. Add the Espagnole sauce and simmer for 10 minutes. Blanch the bone marrow pieces for 1–2 minutes, then drain. Add the bone marrow and chopped parsley to the sauce just before serving.

SAUCE BORDELAISE 2

(a very special sauce for steak)
Cooking time 8–10 minutes Makes 450 ml/¾ pint

METRIC/IMPERIAL

2 tablespoons chopped onion
½ carrot, finely sliced
2 cloves garlic, crushed
25 g/1 oz butter
25 g/1 oz flour
450 ml/¾ pint beef stock
½ bay leaf
2 tablespoons chopped ham
2 tablespoons chopped parsley
8 peppercorns
1 tablespoon Worcestershire sauce
1 tablespoon tomato ketchup
2 tablespoons dry sherry

Sauté the onion, carrot and garlic in the butter and stir in the flour, until the mixture is lightly browned. Add all the remaining ingredients, except the sherry, bring to the boil and simmer for about 10 minutes. Strain the sauce (or liquidise in a blender), add the sherry, season to taste and reheat gently to serve.

SAUCE LYONNAISE

Cooking time 20 minutes Serves 4

METRIC/IMPERIAL

½ Spanish onion, finely chopped
25 g/1 oz butter
6 tablespoons dry white wine
300 ml/½ pint Espagnole sauce (see page 175)
1 tablespoon chopped parsley
1 tablespoon butter

Sauté the onion in butter until golden brown. Add the wine and simmer until it has reduced by half. Add the Espagnole sauce and simmer gently for about 15 minutes, then add the chopped parsley and stir in the butter just before serving.

BROWN ONION SAUCE

Cooking time 20 minutes Makes approximately 300 ml/½ pint

METRIC/IMPERIAL

2 onions, finely chopped
25 g/1 oz butter
150 ml/¼ pint dry white wine
150 ml/¼ pint Espagnole sauce (see page 175)
1 teaspoon finely chopped parsley

Fry the onions in the butter, until golden brown, add the wine and cook until the liquid is reduced by half. Add the Espagnole sauce and simmer for 15 minutes. Just before serving, add the parsley.

This sauce is especially good with left-over meat and vegetables.

ITALIAN TOMATO SAUCE

Cooking time 35 minutes Makes 500 ml/17 fl oz

METRIC/IMPERIAL

2 onions, chopped
2 sticks celery, chopped
few bacon rinds
1 clove garlic, crushed
2 tablespoons oil
1 kg/2 lb ripe tomatoes, fresh or canned
2 tablespoons cornflour
500 ml/17 fl oz water or stock
1 tablespoon brown sugar
½ teaspoon basil
seasoning

Fry the onion, celery, bacon rinds and garlic in the oil for 3–4 minutes, without browning. Add the roughly chopped tomatoes with juice and cook, stirring for 1–2 minutes. Blend the cornflour with a little water. Add with the remaining water, sugar and basil to the pan and bring to the boil. Simmer for about 30 minutes, strain and season to taste.

Variations

For liquidizer owners: Put all the ingredients into a liquidizer and blend on maximum speed for 30 seconds. Simmer for about 15 minutes.

Note

If canned tomatoes are used, it is not necessary to strain the sauce to remove the skins.

SHALLOT SAUCE

Cooking time 10 minutes Serves 4

METRIC/IMPERIAL

6 shallots, finely chopped
15 g/½ oz butter
200 ml/7 fl oz good brown gravy
1 teaspoon lemon juice
½ teaspoon chopped parsley

Fry the shallots in the butter until lightly browned, add the gravy and bring to the boil. Add the remaining ingredients and simmer for 10 minutes, before serving.

BARBECUE SAUCE

Cooking time 30 minutes Serves 4

METRIC/IMPERIAL

50 g/2 oz onion, chopped
50 g/2 oz celery, chopped
25 g/1 oz butter
½ tablespoon plain flour
½ teaspoon paprika
1 teaspoon salt
1 tablespoon lemon juice
150 ml/¼ pint water
50 g/2 oz soft brown sugar
3 tablespoons vinegar
1 green pepper, chopped (optional)
1 tablespoon chilli sauce
1 tablespoon Worcestershire sauce
1 tablespoon tomato ketchup
1 tablespoon made mustard

Lightly fry the onion and celery in the butter. Add all the other ingredients in the order given. Simmer for 30 minutes. Stir occasionally.

Serve with pork chops, pork spare ribs, chicken etc.

FRUITY CURRY SAUCE

Cooking time 25 minutes Makes 500 ml/17 fl oz

METRIC/IMPERIAL

1 tablespoon desiccated coconut
1 large onion, chopped
1 large eating apple, peeled, cored and sliced
2 tablespoons oil
25 g/1 oz flour
1½ tablespoons curry powder
500 ml/17 fl oz juice from canned pineapples, made up with water
50 g/2 oz sultanas
2 pineapple rings, chopped
1 tablespoon tomato purée
1 tablespoon marmalade

Just cover the coconut with boiling water. Leave for 5 minutes, strain and use the resulting coconut milk, discarding the coconut. Fry the onion and apple in the oil for 1–2 minutes. Add the flour and curry powder and cook for 5 minutes. This will be a very dry mixture; keep stirring to prevent burning. Add all the other ingredients, including the coconut milkand bring to the boil, stirring all the time. for at least 25 minutes.

This is not a very hot curry sauce and is good with fish or with hard-boiled eggs. Hard-boil fresh eggs, shell and heat through in the sauce.

SWEET AND SOUR SAUCE

Cooking time 10 minutes Serves 4

METRIC/IMPERIAL

225 g/8 oz canned pineapple
2 small carrots, thinly sliced
1 green pepper, seeded and sliced
1 tablespoon cornflour
1 tablespoon brown sugar
2–3 teaspoons soy sauce
2 tablespoons olive oil
2–3 teaspoons vinegar
3–4 pickled onions, gherkins or mixed pickles

Drain the pineapple juice into a pan; dice the pineapple. Simmer the carrots and pepper in the pineapple juice for 5 minutes. Mix the cornflour, brown sugar, soy sauce, oil and vinegar together. Blend with the pineapple juice in the pan. Bring to the boil and simmer for

3 minutes. Slice the pickles and add with the diced pineapple to the sauce.

SHALLOT SPICER

METRIC/IMPERIAL

600 ml/1 pint inexpensive sherry

100 g/4 oz shallots, finely chopped

Place the chopped shallots in a wide-neck bottle, pour over the sherry and closely cork for 14 days. Strain the liquor into small bottles and cork tightly; store for use. Use a tablespoon or two to liven up an ordinary gravy.

MAYONNAISE

METRIC/IMPERIAL

2 egg yolks
2 tablespoons lemon juice or white wine vinegar
300 ml/½ pint olive oil
seasoning

To make the mayonnaise, all the ingredients should be at room temperature. Beat the egg yolks until they are thick and creamy, add a teaspoon of the lemon juice, then the oil very gradually, beating each addition until really thick. Finally add the remaining lemon juice and seasoning to taste.

Should the mixture curdle at any stage, use the curdled mixture to start again with another egg yolk.

Using a high speed electric blender makes easy work of making excellent mayonnaise.

Variation

Add 2–3 tablespoons of chopped chives for chive mayonnaise.

TARTARE SAUCE

Mayonaise
Chives
Parsley
Tarragon
Capers

Combine the mayonnaise with the other ingredients, finely chopped, in quantities to suit personal taste.

GARLIC MAYONNAISE

(sometimes called Aioli sauce)
Makes about 150 ml/¼ pint

METRIC/IMPERIAL

2 egg yolks
3 large cloves garlic, crushed
7–8 tablespoons olive oil
1 teaspoon lemon juice
few drops water
salt
freshly milled pepper

Beat the egg yolks and crushed garlic together. Gradually beat in the olive oil, drop by drop, increasing as the mixture begins to thicken. When half the oil has been used, beat in the lemon juice and water. Continue with the remaining oil. Season to taste and serve well chilled. Good with cold fish and beef.

Note
If the sauce should curdle, place another egg yolk in another bowl and beat the curdled sauce into it very, very slowly.

FRENCH DRESSING

Serves 6

METRIC/IMPERIAL

1 teaspoon sugar
½ teaspoon salt
generous pinch black pepper
1 teaspoon chopped chives
5 tablespoons olive oil
2 tablespoons wine vinegar
¼ teaspoon basil

Combine all the ingredients in a screw top jar and shake well.

Note
It is a good idea to make up three or four times the above quantity and store in a refrigerator.

SAGE AND ONION STUFFING

Cooking time 15–20 minutes
Oven temperature Moderate 180°C, 350°F, Gas Mark 4
Serves 4–6

METRIC/IMPERIAL

4 onions, parboiled and finely chopped
40 g/1½ oz butter or margarine
100 g/4 oz white breadcrumbs
2 teaspoons chopped fresh or 1 teaspoon dried sage
½ teaspoon salt
¼ teaspoon pepper
little milk

Sauté the chopped onions in 25 g/1 oz of the butter or margarine, add the breadcrumbs, sage, seasoning and enough milk to make a fairly stiff mixture. Place in a greased shallow ovenproof dish and dot the top with the remaining butter or margarine. Bake until firm and golden brown, or use to stuff pork or poultry.

Note
The author is not adverse to packet sage and onion stuffing, but thinks the product greatly improved by the addition of one finely chopped large fresh onion per packet.

STUFFING FOR FISH

Serves 8

METRIC/IMPERIAL

75g/3 oz butter or margarine, softened
50 g/2 oz white breadcrumbs
2 tablespoons chopped parsley
2 tablespoons chopped chives
1 tablespoon capers
1 teaspoon made mustard
2 cloves garlic, crushed
seasoning

Combine all the ingredients and divide evenly between the fish.
Ideal for mackerel, trout, herrings, codling etc.

ONION AND APPLE STUFFING

Cooking time 35 minutes Serves 6
Oven temperature Moderate 180°C, 350°F, Gas Mark 4

METRIC/IMPERIAL

3 large onions
3 large apples
100 g/4 oz breadcrumbs
seasoning
generous pinch sugar
1 teaspoon chopped sage
25 g/1 oz butter

Peel and chop the onions and cook for about 5 minutes in enough water to cover. Strain, but keep liquor for binding the stuffing. Peel and dice the apples, mix with the onions and breadcrumbs, seasoning, sugar and sage. Bind with a little onion liquor. Lightly grease a shallow dish and spread the stuffing in evenly. Dot with the butter and bake for 30 minutes in a moderate oven.

May be used to stuff poultry or boned joints. Particularly good with pork and duck.

SPRING ONION STUFFING

Serves 4–6 (enough for a 1.75-kg/4-lb chicken)

METRIC/IMPERIAL

1 lemon
100 g/4 oz fresh white breadcrumbs
4 large spring onions, chopped
4 tablespoons chopped parsley
2 teaspoons chopped fresh mint
seasoning
100 g/4 oz butter, melted

Grate the lemon rind, then remove the pith and chop the flesh. Combine all the ingredients with the lemon rind and flesh and use to stuff the neck cavity of a chicken.

WALNUT AND ONION STUFFING

Cooking time 25–30 minutes (if baked separately) Serves 6
Oven temperature Hot 220°C, 425°F, Gas Mark 7

METRIC/IMPERIAL

1 onion, chopped
40 g/1½ oz margarine or butter
100 g/4 oz walnuts, coarsely chopped
100 g/4 oz fresh white breadcrumbs
grated ring of 1 lemon
2 tablespoons mixed herbs, including parsley (fresh, if possible)
½ teaspoon cinnamon
seasoning
1 egg, beaten

Sauté the onion in the fat for about 5 minutes until soft but not browned, add the walnuts and continue cooking for a further 3–4 minutes. Mix the breadcrumbs, lemon rind, herbs, cinnamon and seasoning in a bowl, add the walnut mixture and mix well. Bind with the beaten egg and use to stuff poultry or boned meat, or alternatively bake separately in a greased dish in a hot oven for 15–20 minutes.

ORANGE AND CELERY STUFFING

Cooking time 15–20 minutes Serves 6
Oven temperature Moderate 180°C, 350°F, Gas Mark 4

METRIC/IMPERIAL

1 onion, finely chopped
25 g/1 oz butter or margarine
grated rind of 1 orange
1 onion cube, crumbled
100 g/4 oz fresh breadcrumbs
pinch thyme
2 tablespoons chopped parsley
1 stick celery, finely chopped
seasoning
1 beaten egg

Sauté the onion in the fat. Add all the other ingredients to the onions, binding together with a little beaten egg. Bake separately in a greased shallow ovenproof dish, or use to stuff boned lamb or pork.

FESTIVE STUFFING

Suitable for a 5–6-kg/11–13-lb turkey

METRIC/IMPERIAL

75 g/3 oz butter
1 large onion, finely chopped
1 large cooking apple, finely chopped
150 g/5 oz mushrooms, chopped
350 g/12 oz fresh white breadcrumbs
225 g/8 oz liver sausage, skin removed
225 g/8 oz sausagemeat
6 tablespoons chopped parsley
1 teaspoon ground nutmeg
seasoning

Melt the butter in a large pan and fry the onion and apple for 3 minutes. Add the mushrooms and cook for a further 2 minutes. Remove from the heat and stir in the other ingredients thoroughly.

WHOLE ONION AND PRUNE STUFFING

Use whole, well-seasoned, un-cooked onion with whole apples, soaked prunes, and a bunch of parsley to stuff any poultry.

ONION FLAVOUR FOR VEGETABLES

During cooking add a medium, finely chopped onion to any of the following for additional flavour:

broccoli
curly kale
spring greens
cabbage
peas

Preserves and Pickles

I am indebted to Jill Nice for allowing me to use some of her favourite recipes in this section. Mrs Nice is, to my mind, the veritable queen of preserves of every kind and one day I hope we shall see her thousands of recipes in print. She has also given me the following information, by way of introduction to this section.

A few odds and ends that I have learned during my peregrinations:
I find that garlic is best minced or finely chopped in chutney and relishes, but thinly sliced in pickles. I never use a garlic press.

To pickle onions, I drop them into a pan of boiling water for 1 minute and then transfer them to a bowl of cold water. I peel them under water and always take care not to damage the flesh, for it will discolour. I do not use soft onion in a pickle unless for a specific purpose because it goes flabby. Try to use the firm English onions, rather than the Spanish.

Chives are rarely used in the making of preserves, except for a few herb jellies. They are too delicate to withstand such treatment.

Shallot has a much milder flavour than the all-purpose onion, yet it has more flavour than the Spanish. If a recipe says shallots, then they should be used, particularly when wine or wine vinegar is included – they have a more aromatic quality. Silverskin or button onions are essential for mixed pickles and piccalilli, where the vegetable remains wholly recognizable. Sliced onions tend to go soft.

RAW ONION RELISH

Cooking time 30 minutes Serves 4–6

METRIC/IMPERIAL

2 tablespoons Black Barbados (or Molasses) sugar
6 tablespoons lemon juice
50 g/2 oz fresh mint, finely chopped
2 large onions, thinly sliced
1 large red or green pepper, seeded and thinly sliced

Heat the sugar in the lemon juice until dissolved. Add the chopped mint to the liquor and simmer gently for 30 minutes. Put the onion and pepper slices into a serving bowl. Pour over the minted dressing and chill well before serving.

Excellent with cold beef or lamb.

BLACKBERRY AND BEETROOT CHUTNEY

METRIC/IMPERIAL

1 kg/2¼ lb raw beetroot
1 kg/2¼ lb blackberries
250 g/9 oz cooking apples
250 g/9 oz onions
175 g/6 oz soft brown sugar
175 g/6 oz sultanas
2 teaspoons freshly ground black pepper
15 g/½ oz curry powder
15 g/½ oz ground ginger
150 ml/¼ pint malt vinegar
½ teaspoon mustard
½ teaspoon cayenne pepper
hot, dry sterile jars with non-metal lids

Wash the beetroot and cook without damaging. Peel and roughly chop when cool. Wash and pick over the blackberries. Wash, peel, core and chop the apples and peel and chop the onions. Put all the ingredients into a stainless steel pan, except the mustard and cayenne – mix these two together with one tablespoon of the vinegar and put to one side. Simmer the chutney until quite thick, then add the mustard mixture, stir well and continue to cook until thick enough to pot. Pot. Seal when cold.

Try to use the firm red onions, which are strong, to counteract the sweetness of the blackberries and beetroot. The onion also balances the fiery spices, turning a sweet, really hot chutney into a mellow and fruity mixture that owes much of its pungency to the onion.

CHARITABLE CHUTNEY

METRIC/IMPERIAL

500 g/18 oz prunes
1 kg/2¼ lb green apples
500 g/18 oz cooking pears
500 g/18 oz green tomatoes
500 g/18 oz raisins
225 g/8 oz preserved ginger
450 g/1 lb onions
2 cloves garlic
1 tablespoon sea salt
½ teaspoon cayenne pepper
1.25 kg/2½ lb soft brown sugar
500 ml/17 fl oz brown malt vinegar
hot, dry sterile jars with non-metal lids

Put the prunes in a bowl with a good quantity of water and leave to soften for 4 hours. Drain, remove the stones and mince. Peel, core and mince the apples and pears. Mince the tomatoes, raisins and ginger. Peel and mince the onions and garlic. Put all the ingredients, except the sugar and vinegar, into a large stainless steel pan and bring gently to the boil, stirring all the time. Cover and cook, without burning, for approximately 1½ hours, or until soft. Dissolve the sugar in the vinegar and add it to the fruity mixture. Bring to the boil, stirring constantly, and boil gently and uncovered until it is thick and smooth. Pot and seal.

Use a stronger onion which will not be overwhelmed by the fruity sweetness of the other ingredients. The garlic ensures an underlying suggestion of the savoury. Without either onion or garlic this recipe would lack appeal as a chutney.

It matures well.

SPICY APRICOT CHUTNEY

METRIC/IMPERIAL

450 g/1 lb dried apricots
675 g/1½ lb onions
2 cloves garlic
2 oranges
225 g/8 oz seedless raisins
2 teaspoons salt
2 tablespoons mustard powder
½ teaspoon ground mixed spice
900 ml/1½ pints cider vinegar
450 g/1 lb white sugar
6 hot, dry, sterile jars with
non-metal lids

Wash and chop the apricots and leave to soak overnight in a deep bowl, well covered with water. The next day drain the apricots. Peel and chop the onions and garlic. Grate the rinds and squeeze the juice from the oranges. Put all the ingredients, except the vinegar and sugar, into a stainless steel pan and bring gently to the boil. Cover and simmer gently for 30 minutes. Put the vinegar into a stainless steel saucepan, bring it to the boil and pour it over the sugar, stir well to dissolve. Add this sweet vinegar to the chutney, stir well and continue to cook uncovered for a further hour. Continue to stir from time to time to ensure that it does not burn. When it is nice and thick, it has cooked sufficiently. Pot and seal immediately.

Mild Spanish onions are preferred for this recipe, in which they blend nicely with the fruit without being overwhelming. The moderate use of garlic brings out the best in all the ingredients, particularly the oranges. A happy combination.

PINEAPPLE RELISH

METRIC/IMPERIAL

1 kg/2¼ lb prepared pineapple
50 g/2 oz sea salt
8–12 cloves garlic
175 g/6 oz fresh ginger root
400 g/14 oz seedless raisins
300 g/11 oz soft light brown or
white sugar
600 ml/1 pint brown or white
malt vinegar
½ teaspoon freshly grated
nutmeg
hot dry sterile jars with
non-metal lids

Peel the pineapple, remove the hard core, chop and weigh the flesh. Lay it on a dish and sprinkle with the sea salt. Leave to stand for 1–2 hours. Peel and mince the garlic and ginger. Mince the raisins. Turn the pineapple into a colander, drain and rinse with a little extra vinegar, shake dry. Place the sugar and vinegar in a stainless steel pan and bring to the boil, simmer for 10 minutes and then add the pineapple and all the other ingredients, stir well and simmer gently until the relish is thick and smooth. Pot and seal. The whole purpose of this recipe is the rapport established between the garlic and pineapple. The garlic is obvious but it gains a strange quality from the sharp distinctive flavour of the pineapple; this is also brought out by the use of the salt.

Keep for 2 weeks before using.

APPLE AND ONION PICKLE

METRIC/IMPERIAL

1 kg/2¼ lb cooking apples
1 kg/2¼ lb onions
175 g/6 oz sultanas
25 g/1 oz peppercorns
25 g/1 oz cloves
75 g/3 oz dried chillies
1 litre/1¾ pints malt vinegar
1 tablespoon salt
hot, dry, sterile, wide-necked jars with non-metal lids

Wash, peel, core and chop the apples into very small pieces. Peel and shred the onions. Wash the sultanas and mix well with the onions and apples. Fill the jars with the mixture. Tie the spices in a muslin bag and put in a saucepan with the vinegar and salt. Bring to the boil. Take it off the heat, cover and allow to stand for 30 minutes. Remove the lid and bring to the boil again, simmer for 10 minutes. Strain and pour over the contents of the jars, making sure that they are well covered. Seal.

This is a quick pickle to make, but should be left for at least a month to mature before eating.

Use a strong crisp onion which will hold its own against the chilli and which will stay crisp on keeping, thus improving the bite and texture of this pickle.

PICKLED BEANS

METRIC/IMPERIAL

- 1 kg/2¼ lb green beans
- 225 g/8 oz shallots or small silverskin onions
- 300 ml/½ pint vinegar
- 300 ml/½ pint dry cider
- 2 teaspoons salt
- 1 tablespoon dill seeds
- ½ teaspoon cayenne pepper
- ½ teaspoon turmeric
- 225 g/8 oz soft light brown sugar
- 4 hot, dry sterile jars with non-metal lids

Wash, top and tail and, if necessary, string the beans. Cook in a pan of boiling salted water until just tender, not flabby, otherwise they will spoil the pickle. Drain them well and pack into the jars, keep warm. Wash and peel the onions and put them with all the other ingredients except the sugar, into a stainless steel pan. Bring to the boil and add the sugar, stirring well until it has dissolved. Bring to the boil again for a further 3 minutes. Pour over the beans, making sure that there are no air bubbles and that the beans are completely covered with vinegar. Seal.

Keep for a least 2 months.

It is preferable to use the silverskin onions which are tiny, white, quite strong and slightly sweet – they do not transmit their flavour to the beans as would a large cooking onion. They also stay crisp.

PICKLED PEARS, APPLES AND GREEN TOMATOES

METRIC/IMPERIAL

- 2 litres/3½ pints white wine vinegar
- 12 fresh tarragon sprigs
- 24 tiny silverskin onions
- 2 dried red chillies
- 16 cloves
- 20 black peppercorns
- 6 garlic cloves
- 25 g/1 oz sea salt
- 100 g/4 oz white sugar
- 1 kg/2¼ lb pears
- 1 kg/2¼ lb green apples
- 500 g/18 oz very small green tomatoes
- hot, dry sterile preserving jars

Put the vinegar, tarragon, skinned onions, chillies, cloves, peppercorns, peeled and finely chopped garlic, salt and sugar into a stainless steel pan and bring to the boil. Simmer for 10 minutes and remove from the heat. Peel, core and cut the pears and apples into quarters. Put into a saucepan with just enough water to cover and cook gently until well cooked but completely firm. Wipe the tomatoes and prick at the leaf end. Put the fruit and tomatoes into the jars. Bring the vinegar to the boil again and pour it over the fruit to cover completely, make sure that it is not strained and that the spices, herbs and onions are added to the jar and that there are no air bubbles. Seal.

The small onions once again retain their own flavour without imparting it too strongly to the other fruit. The garlic combines with the herbs and spices to provide a well-balanced flavour.

Leave for 1 month before eating.

MARINATED AUBERGINES

METRIC/IMPERIAL

1 kg/2¼ lb aubergines
sea salt
300 ml/½ pint white wine vinegar
6 cloves garlic
1 tablespoon dried oregano
olive, corn or sunflower oil
large dry, clean glass preserving jars

Wash, peel and slice the aubergines. Arrange them in a large nylon sieve or colander and sprinkle with a little sea salt on each layer as you go. Leave for 4 hours. Shake occasionally to allow the juices to drain away, these are rather bitter and not an asset to a pickle. Put the vinegar in a stainless steel pan with the aubergine slices and add just enough water to cover, if necessary. Poach gently for 5 minutes. Drain well. Crush the garlic. Now place the aubergine slices in the jar, alternating each layer with a sprinkled mixture of the garlic and oregano, not with a heavy hand, otherwise it won't go all the way. When the jars are full cover the contents completely with the oil and seal it tightly.

Keep a week before using, but it then has a long storage life. This is an unusual recipe from the sunny Mediterranean. Garlic and oregano combine together to give a rather meaty taste to the bland and fleshy aubergine.

PONTACKS SAUCE

METRIC/IMPERIAL

1 kg/2¼ lb very ripe elderberries
2 tablespoons black peppercorns
1 litre/1¾ pints red wine vinegar, or red wine (claret)
225 g/8 oz shallots
2 teaspoons sea salt
2 blades mace
1 teaspoon whole cloves
2 large pieces root ginger
hot, dry sterile bottles with corks

Wash the berries, removing the stalks if necessary, and put them into an earthenware casserole with the peppercorns. Boil up the vinegar or wine and pour it over the fruit, cover with a lid and put the casserole in a warm oven overnight. The next day peel and mince the shallots and put them with the salt, spices and ginger into a stainless steel pan, add the strained juice from the elderberries and bring to the boil. Boil gently for about 10 minutes. Remove from the heat, cover and allow to cool. Strain carefully, return the sauce to a clean pan, return to the boil just once more. Bottle and seal.

A very good elderberry sauce which is excellent with fish and offal; try a dash in casseroled liver and bacon. Reputation has it that it may be kept for 7 years. Substitute the wine vinegar or red wine for malt vinegar, if economy imposes.

Shallots, because of their mild yet distinctive flavour, are a necessity for this recipe – elderberry juice is a harsh juice which requires the shallot to bring out the gentle side of its nature. A stronger onion would also combine unfavourably with the red wine or vinegar, destroying the subtle yet rich composition.

HOT ONION SAUCE

METRIC/IMPERIAL

1 kg/2¼ lb onions
675 g/1½ lb red plums
40 g/1½ oz sultanas
4 chillies
piece root ginger
600 ml/1 pint malt vinegar
1 tablespoon ground allspice
1½ tablespoons mustard powder
2 teaspoons turmeric powder
2 teaspoons freshly grated nutmeg
175 g/6 oz brown sugar
3 tablespoons sea salt
hot, dry sterile bottles with corks

Peel and chop the onions, wash and stone the plums, chop the sultanas, shred the chillies and bruise the ginger. Put all of these together into a stainless steel pan with half of the vinegar, bring to the boil and then simmer until very soft. Mix the allspice, mustard, turmeric and nutmeg to a smooth paste with a little of the remaining vinegar. Pass the contents of the pan through a fine sieve and return the purée to the clean pan, heat gently and add the spiced paste, sugar and salt. Stir in the remaining vinegar and bring to the boil, stirring well until the sugar has dissolved. Simmer for approximately 20 minutes. Leave until cold.

Bottle and seal.

Excellent with cold meat.

The onions should be strong enough to give balance to the red plums which are usually of a good flavour. The strong spices and seasonings are absorbed by the onion, making it hot and spicy but not rough.

PICKLED ONIONS

There are several ways of pickling onions, but for the best possible results use pickling onions, peel them under cold water, lay them out on a dish and sprinkle with rock or sea salt and leave overnight. Rinse well under cold water and dry well. Pack them into a jar and cover with one of the cold spiced vinegars below.

Leave at least 1 month before opening.

Mild

METRIC/IMPERIAL

1 litre/1¾ pints brown malt vinegar
2 tablespoons mustard seed
2 tablespoons whole cloves
2 tablespoons black peppercorns
2 tablespoons whole allspice
2 tablespoon dried red chillies

Boil all together in a stainless steel pan, and strain if you require a particularly mild pickle.

Hot and Spicy

METRIC/IMPERIAL

1 litre/1¾ pints brown malt vinegar
1 tablespoon black peppercorns
large piece root ginger
1 teaspoon coriander seed
dried chillies
bay leaves

Boil the vinegar, peppercorns, ginger and coriander together in a stainless steel pan. Strain before using. Pack the chillies and bay leaves into the jar with the onions.

Very Hot

METRIC/IMPERIAL

1 litre/1¾ pints white malt vinegar
1 piece ginger root
2 tablespoons grated horseradish
1 tablespoon black peppercorns

Boil all together in a stainless steel pan. Whether you strain it or not before using is up to you.

Note
Silverskin onions should be pickled in a white vinegar and any of the following seasonings may be used: basil, nutmeg, celery seed, chilli, dill, chervil, rosemary.

MIXED PICKLE

Most vinegars used in vegetable pickles are spicy in varying degrees. The first vinegar is flavoured mildly with shallot, the second more pungently with garlic; either vinegar alters the character of the pickle quite considerably.

A mild vinegar

METRIC/IMPERIAL

50 g/2 oz shallots
1 litre/1¾ pints white or brown malt vinegar
25 g/1 oz mustard seed
1 tablespoon mixed pickling spice

Peel and chop the shallots and put with the remaining ingredients into a stainless steel pan. Bring to the boil and boil vigorously for 5 minutes. Remove from the heat, cover and leave for 2 hours. Strain before using.

A hot vinegar

METRIC/IMPERIAL

1 tablespoon mustard powder
1 litre/1¾ pints white vinegar
2 cloves garlic
2 teaspoons sea salt
few dried red chillies

Mix the mustard powder with a little of the vinegar. Peel and chop the garlic. Put all the ingredients, including the mustard paste into a stainless steel pan and bring to the boil. Boil for 5 minutes. Cover and remove from the heat. Leave for 2 hours and then strain through double muslin before using. Retrieve the chillies and keep them in reserve to add to each jar of pickle as you cover with vinegar.

Vegetables to use:
silverskin or shallot onions – peeled
small gherkins – left whole
nasturtium seeds – brine blanched
radish pods – brine blanched
courgettes – unpeeled, thickly sliced
small scarlet runner beans – left whole
cauliflower – in florets
carrot – peeled and cut in fine slices
peppers – cut in short thick strips
dry sterile jars with non-metal lids
Prepare the vegetables and pack them into the jars. Cover with the cold, strained vinegar.

GOOSEBERRY AND GARLIC PICKLE

METRIC/IMPERIAL

1 kg/2¼ lb unripe gooseberries
225 g/8 oz soft brown sugar
500 ml/17 fl oz white wine vinegar
225 g/8 oz mustard seed (or 1 tablespoon mustard powder)
150 g/5 oz garlic
1 teaspoon cayenne pepper
1 tablespoon ground black pepper
350 g/12 oz seedless raisins
sea salt
hot, dry sterile jars with non-metal lids

Wash, top and tail the gooseberries and put them into a stainless steel pan with the sugar and half the vinegar. Heat gently, stirring well, until the sugar has dissolved. Bring to the boil and then simmer until the fruit is soft. Grind and pound the mustard seed, garlic and cayenne together in a bowl and add to the pan with the black pepper and raisins. Stir in the remaining vinegar and bring to the boil, boil hard for 5 minutes, stirring well. Add salt to taste. Pot and seal.

Keep this pungent, strong pickle at least 6 months before using, when it will be guaranteed to take your head off. Garlic is used very frequently with gooseberries and in this particular recipe it gives warmth to the sharpness of the fruit and mellowness to a hot rich mixture.

BITTER LEMON PICKLE

METRIC/IMPERIAL

1 kg/2¼ lb small thin-skinned lemons
2 tablespoons sea salt
450 g/1 lb sultanas
25 g/1 oz fresh root ginger
4 cloves garlic
25 g/1 oz fresh horseradish
1 teaspoon chilli powder
300 ml/½ pint cider vinegar
675 g/1½ lb soft light brown sugar
small, hot, dry sterile jars with non-metal lids

Wash the lemons and, working on a large dish, cut into eighths lengthwise; remove the pips as you go. Sprinkle with salt and leave in the fridge for 2 days, turning over and giving a good stir every now and again. Wash and dry the sultanas, peel the ginger if necessary, peel the garlic and wash and scrape the horseradish. Drain the lemons and reserve the liquid. Put all these ingredients through a coarse mincer and transfer them into a stainless steel pan; add the lemon liquid, chilli powder, vinegar and sugar. Mix well and heat gently, stirring all the time. When the sugar has dissolved, bring to the boil and simmer until thick and soft. Pot and seal.

This is the finest pickle recipe I know, electrifying pungent and aromatic, without being harsh. It is excellent with fish and cheese.

Garlic with lemons and horseradish is an extraordinary combination, which I find impossible to describe, but it *can* only be accomplished *with* garlic.

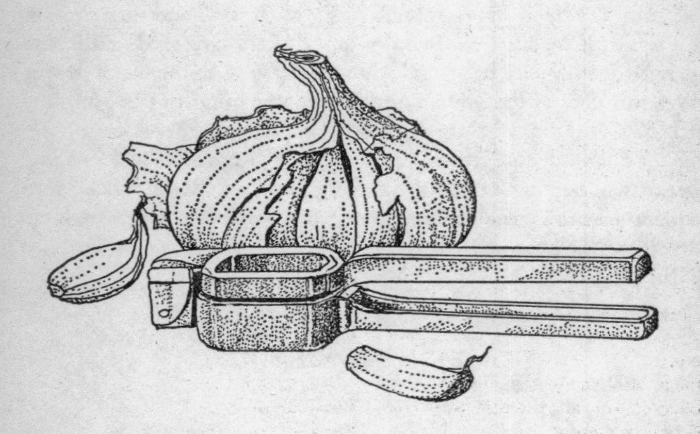

Index

Aigrettes 163
American chicken casserole 105
Anchovy-topped pizza 172
Appetisers and starters 35–45
Apple:
Apple and chive bread 165
Apple and onion pickle 190
Curried apple soup 49
Leek and apple salad 130
Pickled pears, apples and green tomatoes 191
Pork and apple casserole 81
Pork and apple pie 84
Apricot chutney, spicy 189
Aubergine:
Aubergine pâté 35
Marinated aubergines 192
Mediterranean bake 65
Moussaka 75–6
Australian meat and potato pie 74
Avocado:
Avocado appetiser 40
Avocado vichyssoise 50
Chive stuffed avocados, 41

Bacon:
Bacon and banana kebabs 45
Bacon and corn casserole 91
Bacon provençal 87
Burning love 88
Cottage cheese and bacon pudding 88
Danish pie 90
Leek and bacon pie 89
Leek and bacon tartlets 153
Leek pie 89
Onion, bacon and apple pie 153
Onion, bacon and raisin bread 167
Baked onions 113
Bami 81
Banana:
Bacon and banana kebabs 45
Barbados starter 42
Barbecue sauce 178
Bean:
Broad beans with yogurt 122
Paprika beans 122
Pickled beans 191
Béchamel sauce 174
Beef:
Australian meat and potato pie 74
Beef bourguignonne 70
Beef in red wine 66
Boeuf strogonoff 68
Braised beef with chestnuts 69
Carbonnade of beef 69
Chilli con carne 77
Chinese pepper steak 71
Goulash 67
Hamburger pie 150
Homespun loaf 78
Moussaka 75–6
North Country potato hot-pot 77
Nutty 'burgers 78
Ragoût of beef 65
Spicy meat kebabs 74
Suki yaki 71
Swiss steak special 72
Tasty steak 73
Worcester country casserole 67
Beer sausage bake 100
Beetroot soup (Bortscht) 56
Blackberry and beetroot chutney 187
Blue cheese dressing 131
Boeuf strogonoff 68
Bordelaise sauce 175–6
Bortsch 56
Bouillabaisse 61
Bread:
Apple and chive bread 165
Basic bread recipe 166–7
Cheese and onion smørhorn 169
French onion bread 168
Gardener's tea bread 165
Garlic bread 168
Onion, bacon and raisin bread 167

Bread—*continued*
  Orange, garlic and parsley bread 167
  Provençale loaf 165
  Walnut, cheese and chive bread 167
Broad beans with yogurt 122
Burning love 88
Butter Bercy 141
Butters, savoury 139–41

Cabbage:
  Cabbage with onion 119
  Hot vegetable slaw 123
Canapés 137, 138
Carbonnade of beef 69
Carrot:
  Carrot soup 53
  Spring time onions with baby carrots 111
Cassoulet 86
Cauliflower, spicy 121
Celeriac with chive mayonnaise 134
Celery:
  Braised celery with onions and walnuts 120
Charitable chutney 188
Cheese. *See also* Cottage cheese
  Cheese and garlic scones 159
  Cheese-onion ball canapés 137
  Cheese and onion smørhorn 169
  Cheese and onion soup 54
  Cheese and onion sticks 139
  Cheese and onion twirls 156
  Cheese sauce 174
  Cheese shortcrust pastry 156
  Cheese soufflé with garlic croûtons 145
  Cracker cheese flan 151
  Golden layer pudding 162
  Onion-cheese pinwheel canapés 138
  Onion and cheese salad 129
  Onion and cheese spread 141
  Onion-cheese squares 148
  Walnut, cheese and chive bread 167
Chestnuts, braised beef with 69
Chicken:
  American chicken casserole 105
  Chicken and egg balls 138
  Chicken in a parcel 104
  Chicken pimento 102
  Chicken salamagundy 131
  Hawaiian chicken 106
  Norwegian hot-pot 107
  Quick chicken provençal 104
  Roast garlic chicken 105
  Tandoori-style chicken 103
Chilli con carne 77
Chinese leeks 118
Chinese pepper steaks 71
Chives 12, 14:
  To freeze chives 23
  To grow chives 17
  To prepare and use chives 31
  Chilled cucumber and chive soup 54
  Chive butter 140
  Chive mayonnaise 135
  Chive stuffed avocados 41
  Chives and cucumber – hot 119
  Flaky pastry with chives 157
  Scones with chives 160
  Suet crust pastry with chives 159
Choux pastry 158
Chutneys 187–9
Cider, leeks in 86
Cider, spicy sausage in 102
Cock-a-leekie soup 49
Cold spring soup 55
Corn:
  Bacon and corn casserole 91
  Corn chowder 47
  Sweetcorn and spring onion salad 132
Cottage Cheese:
  Cottage cheese d'Artois 161
  Cottage cheese and bacon pudding 88
  Cottage cheese and garlic dip 142
  Savoury puffs 162
Country garden flan 154
Country soup 56
Courgette:
  Courgette and leek salad 133
  Courgettes and onion starter 43
  Onion and courgette bake 119

Cream of leek and rice soup 57
Cream of onion soup 48
Croûtons, garlic 139
Cucumber:
  Chilled cucumber and chive soup 54
  Chives and cucumber – hot 119
Curried apple soup 49
Curried onion omelette 145
Curry sauce, fruity 179

Danish marinated herrings 38
Danish pie 90
Devilled kidney gougère 163
Devon pie 80
Dips 142–3

Egg:
  Cheese soufflé with garlic croûtons 145
  Chicken and egg balls 138
  Curried onion omelette 145
  Onion and egg spread 142
Elderberry:
  Pontacks sauce 193
Espagnole sauce 175

Faggots 97
Festive stuffing 185
Fish. *See also* Herring etc.
  Bouillabaisse 61
  Fish patties 149
  Fish plaki 62
  Fish soup 57
  Pickled curried fish 39
  Stuffing for fish 182
Flaky pastry 157; with chives 157
Flans *see* Tarts etc.
French dressing 181
French onion bread 168
Fruity curry sauce 179

Gardener's casserole 99
Gardener's tea bread 165
Garlic 11, 12, 14:
  To grow garlic 19
  To prepare and use garlic 32
  To store garlic 21
  Blender garlic dip 143
  Cheese and garlic scones 159
  Choux pastry with garlic 158
  Garlic bread 168
  Garlic bread strips 139
  Garlic butter 140
  Garlic and cottage cheese dip 142
  Garlic croûtons 139
  Garlic mayonnaise 181
  Garlic olives 144
  Garlic pastry 156
  Garlic potatoes 125
  Gooseberry and garlic pickle 197
  Roast garlic chicken 105
Gazpacho 59
Glazed onions 110
Golden layer pudding 162
Gooseberry and garlic pickle 197
Goulash 67
Grapefruit:
  Onion and grapefruit salad 129
Green salad with Blue cheese dressing 131

Ham and onion spread 141
Hamburger pie 150
Hawaiian chicken 106
Herby herrings 39
Herring:
  Danish marinated herrings 38
  Herby herrings 39
Homespun loaf 78
Honey baked pork chops 85

Iced onion rings 145
Indian salad 136
Indian sole knots 62

Jambalaya 83

Kebabs:
  Bacon and banana kebabs 45
  Spicy meat kebabs 74
Kidney:
  Casserole ox kidneys 92
  Devilled kidney gougère 163
  Kidney, potato and onion pie 93
  Kidneys and baby onions 94
  Onions and kidney dumplings 95
Kipper star pie 63

Lamb:
- Devon pie 80
- Lamb chops in parcels 79
- Lamb paprika 79
- Moussaka 76

Lambs' tongues, leeks with 92

Leeks 10, 14:
- To freeze leeks 23
- To grow leeks 18
- Basic cooking methods 29–30
- Braised leeks 116
- Chinese leeks 118
- Cock-a-leekie soup 49
- Courgette and leek salad 133
- Cream of leek and rice soup 57
- Crispy-coated leeks 117
- Devon pie 80
- Leek and apple salad 130
- Leek and bacon pie 89
- Leek and bacon tartlets 153
- Leek and liver hot-pot 96
- Leek and liver sausage hot-pot 98
- Leek pie 89
- Leek and potato soup 53
- Leek salad starter 44
- Leek and salmon soup 58
- Leek and shrimp salad 130
- Leeks in cider 86
- Leeks in cream 117
- Leeks au gratin 146
- Leeks with Lambs' tongues 92
- Leeks with red wine 115
- Leeks with rice 115
- Leeks in soured cream 116
- Microwave cooked leeks 33
- Nutritive value of leeks 15
- Peking leeks 44
- Pork with leeks 85
- Swiss leek with sausage 101
- Vichyssoise 52

Lemon:
- Bitter lemon pickle 197

Liver:
- Faggots 97
- Leek and liver hot pot 96
- Liver Italian 96
- Liver sausage pâté 36
- Orangey liver 97

Lyonnaise sauce 176

Mayonnaise 180

Mediterranean bake 65

Microwave cooking 33, 111–12

Middle East vegetable salad 135

Mixed pickle 195

Mrs Beeton's onion salad 127

Moussaka 75–6

Mushroom:
- Barbados starter 42
- Mushrooms with chive mayonnaise 135

Normandy potatoes 124

Norwegian hot-pot 107

Nutty 'burgers 78

Onion 9–10, 13:
- To chop onions 25, 27
- To cook onions (basic methods) 25–9
- To freeze onions 22–3
- To grow onions 17–18
- To slow cook onions 33
- To store onions 21
- Apple and onion pickle 190
- Baked onions 113
- Braised celery with onions and walnuts 120
- Brown onion sauce 177
- Cabbage with onions 119
- Cheese-onion ball canapés 137
- Cheese and onion soup 54
- Cheese and onion sticks 139
- Cheese and onion twirls 156
- Choux pastry with onion 158
- Country soup 56
- Courgettes and onion starter 43
- Cream of onion soup 48
- Crispy onion circles 109
- Curried onion omelette 145
- Deep-fried onion rings 113
- Dried onion rings 22
- French onion bread 168
- Glazed onions 110
- Grilled onion slices 114
- Ham and onion spread 141
- Hot onion sauce 193
- Iced onion rings 145
- Kidney, potato and onion pie 93

Kidneys and baby onions 94
Marinated onions 144
Mediterranean bake 65
Microwave baked onions 111
Microwave buttery onions 112
Mrs Beeton's onion salad 127
Nutritive value of onions 15
Onion and apple stuffing 183
Onion, bacon and apple pie 153
Onion, bacon and raisin bread 167
Onion butter 140
Onion-cheese pinwheel canapés 138
Onion and cheese salad 129
Onion and cheese spread 141
Onion cheese squares 148
Onion and courgette bake 119
Onion and egg spread 142
Onion flavour for vegetables 185
Onion and grapefruit salad 129
Onion and green pepper soup 50
Onion and parsnip soup 51
Onion pastry 156
Onion and pepper küchen 164
Onion and potato ring 148
Onion pudding 64
Onion ragoût 114
Onion sauce, basic 174
Onion scones 159
Onion soup – French style 47
Onion starter from Monaco 43
Onion tart 152
Onion and walnut loaf 147
Onions in cream 144
Onions à la grecque 127
Onions and kidney dumplings 95
Onions roasted in foil 114
Party onions 143
Pickled onions 194–5
Quick onion küchen 150
Raw onion relish 187
Scalloped onions 144
Soufflé onion soup 48
Spring time onions with baby carrots 111
Sprouts with onions 121
Stuffed onions 112
Swiss potatoes and onions 125
Tomato and onion casserole 120
Tomatoes and onions in foil 114
Tripe and onions 95
Whole onion and prune stuffing 185

Orange:
- Orange and celery stuffing 184
- Orange garlic and parsley bread 167
- Orangey liver 97

Sausages in orange sauce 101
Tomato and orange soup 52
Ox kidneys casserole 92

Paprika beans 122
Pastry:
- Cheese shortcrust pastry 156
- Choux pastry 158
- Flaky pastry 157
- Garlic pastry 156
- Onion pastry 156
- Shortcrust pastry 156
- Suet crust pastry 158–9

Pâté:
- Aubegine pâté 35
- Liver sausage pâté 36
- Pâté dip 142
- Pâté for springtime 37
- Taramasalata 37, 38

Peanut soup 51
Pears, apples and green tomatoes, pickled 191
Peking leeks 44
Pepper, red or green:
- Chinese pepper steak 71
- Onion and green pepper soup 50
- Onion and pepper küchen 164
- Pepper slaw 134

Pickled curried fish 39
Pickles 190, 194–8
Pies:
- Australian meat and potato pie 74
- Danish pie 90
- Devon pie 80
- Hamburger pie 150
- Kidney, potato and onion pie 93
- Kipper star pie 63
- Leek and bacon pie 89
- Leek pie 89
- Onion, bacon and apple pie 153

Pies—*continued*
Poacher's pie 108
Pork and apple pie 84
Pineapple relish 189
Pissaladière 160
Pizza 170–2; mock 172
Poacher's pie 108
Pontacks sauce 193
Pork:
Bami 81
Economy cassoulet 86
Honey bakes pork chops 85
Jambalaya 83
Pork and apple casserole 81
Pork and apple pie 84
Pork with leeks 85
Thatched pork casserole 82
Potato:
Australian meat and potato pie 74
Avocado vichyssoise 50
Californian potato salad 133
Country soup 56
Garlic potatoes 125
Kidney, potato and onion pie 93
Leek and potato soup 33
Normandy potatoes 124
North Country potato hot-pot 77
Onion and potato ring 148
Potato bake 147
Potato-cream bake 126
Potatoes mexicano 124
Sausage supper 98
Swiss potatoes and onions 125
Vichyssoise 52
Prawns in garlic mayonnaise 40
Preserves and pickles 186–98
Pressure cooking 34
Provençale loaf 165
Puddings:
Cottage cheese and bacon pudding 88
Golden layer pudding 162
Onion pudding 64

Rabbit:
Poacher's pie 108
Rabbit sauté 107
Ragoût of beef 65
Ratatouille 123
Relishes 187, 189
Rice:
Leeks with rice 115
Soy rice 126

Sage and onion stuffing 182
Sage and onion suet crust pastry 159
Salads:
Californian potato salad 133
Celeriac with chive mayonnaise 134
Chicken salamagundy 131
Courgette and leek salad 133
Green salad with Blue cheese dressing 131
Indian salad 136
Leek and apple salad 130
Leek salad starter 44
Leek and shrimp salad 130
Middle East vegetable salad 135
Mrs Beeton's onion salad 127
Mushrooms with chive mayonnaise 135
Onion and cheese salad 129
Onion and grapefruit salad 129
Onions à la grecque 127
Pepper slaw 134
Spanish salad 136
Sweetcorn and spring onion salad 132
Tomato salad 132
Yorkshire salad 132
Sauces:
Barbecue sauce 178
Béchamel sauce 174
Cheese sauce 174
Chive mayonnaise 135
Espagnole sauce 175
French dressing 181
Fruity curry sauce 179
Garlic mayonnaise 181
Hot onion sauce 193
Italian tomato sauce 177
Mayonnaise 180
Onion sauce, basic, 174
Onion sauce, brown 177
Pontacks sauce 193
Sauce bordelaise 175–6

Sauce lyonnaise 176
Shallot sauce 178
Shallot spicer 180
Sweet and sour sauce 179
Tartare sauce 180
White sauce, basic 173
Sausage:
Beer sausage bake 100
Gardener's casserole 99
Leek and liver sausage hot-pot 98
Sausage risotto 100
Sausauge supper 98
Sausages in orange sauce 101
Spicy sausage in cider 102
Swiss leek with sausage 101
Savouries *see* Snacks and savouries
Savoury butters 139–41
Savoury puffs 162
Scalloped onions 144
Scones 159–60
Seafood bisque 58
Seafood casserole 63
Shallot:
To freeze shallots 23
To grow shallots 18
To prepare and use shallots 31
To store shallots 21
Bacon and banana kebabs 45
Shallot sauce 178
Shallot spicer 180
Shortcrust pastry 156
Shrimp rissoles 149
Snacks and savouries 137–54
Sole:
Indian sole knots 62
Soufflé onion soup 48
Soup:
Avocado vichyssoise 50
Bortsch 56
Carrot soup 53
Cheese and onion soup 54
Chilled cucumber and chive soup 54
Cock-a-leekie soup 49
Cold spring soup 55
Corn chowder 47
Country soup 56
Cream of leek and rice soup 57
Cream of onion soup 48
Curried apple soup 49
Different tomato soup 55
Fish soup 57
Gazpacho 59
Leek and potato soup 53
Leek and salmon soup 58
Onion and green pepper soup 50
Onion and parsnip soup 51
Onion soup – French style 47
Peanut soup 51
Seafood bisque 58
Soufflé onion soup 48
Tomato and orange soup 52
Vichyssoise 52
Soured cream, leeks in 116
Soy rice 126
Spanish salad 136
Spicy apricot chutney 189
Spicy cauliflower 121
Spicy meat kebabs 74
Spicy sausage in cider 102
Spring onion 12:
To grow spring onions 19
To prepare spring onions 31
Nutritive value 15
Scones with spring onions 160
Spring onion and butter 141
Spring onion and cress quiche 151
Spring onion stuffing 183
Spring onion tops savoury 144
Spring onions à la King 118
Sweetcorn and spring onion salad 132
Sprouts with onions 121
Starters and appetisers 35–45
Steak *see* Beef
Stuffed onions 112
Stuffed tomatoes 41
Stuffing:
Festive stuffing 185
Onion and apple stuffing 183
Orange and celery stuffing 184
Sage and onion stuffing 182
Spring onion stuffing 183
Stuffing for fish 182
Walnut and onion stuffing 184
Whole onion and prune stuffing 185
Suet crust pastry 158–9

Suki yaki 71
Sweet and sour sauce 179
Swiss leek with sausage 101
Swiss potatoes and onions 125
Swiss steak special 72

Tandoori-style chicken 103
Taramasalata 37, 38
Tartare sauce 180
Tarts and flans:
  Country garden flan 154
  Cracker cheese flan 151
  Leek and bacon tartlets 153
  Onion tart 152
  Pissaladière 160
  Spring onion and cress quiche 151
Tomato:
  Italian tomato sauce 177
  Stuffed tomatoes 41
  Tomato and onion casserole 120
  Tomato salad 132
  Tomatoes and onions in foil 114
  Tunisian vegetables 42
Tripe and onions 95
Tunisian vegetables 42

Veal cacciatore 91
Vegetable. *See also* Aubergine etc.
  Cold spring soup 55
  Hot vegetable slaw 123
  Middle East vegetable salad 135
  Onion flavour for vegetables 185
  Ratatouille 123
  Tunisian vegetables 42
Vichyssoise 52
Vinegar for pickles 196

Walnut:
  Braised celery with onions and walnuts 120
  Onion and walnut loaf 147
  Walnut, cheese and chive bread 167
  Walnut and onion stuffing 184
White sauce 173–4
Wild garlic 12
Worcestershire country casserole 67

Yogurt:
  Broad beans with yoghurt 122
Yorkshire salad 132

Prices and postage and packing rates shown below were correct at the time of going to press.

FICTION

All prices shown are exclusive of postage and packing.

GENERAL FICTION

☐ THE AFFAIR OF NINA B.	Simmel	£1.20
☐ H.M.S. BOUNTY	John Maxwell	£1.00
☐ TY-SHAN BAY	R. T. Aundrews	95p
☐ A SEA CHANGE	Lois Gould	80p
☐ THE PLAYERS	Gary Brandner	95p
☐ MR. FITTON'S COMMISSION	Showell Styles	85p
☐ CRASH LANDING	Mark Regan	95p
☐ SUMMER LIGHTNING	Judith Richards	£1.00
☐ THE HALO JUMP	Alistair Hamilton	£1.00
☐ SUMMERBLOOD	Anne Rudeen	£1.25
☐ PLACE OF THE DAWN	Gordon Taylor	90p
☐ EARTHLY POSSESSIONS	Anne Tyler	95p
☐ THE MASTER MECHANIC	I. G. Broat	£1.50
☐ THE MEXICAN PROPOSITION (Western)	Matt Chisholm	75p

CRIME/THRILLER

☐ THE TREMOR OF FORGERY	Patricia Highsmith	80p
☐ STRAIGHT	Steve Knickmeyer	80p
☐ THE COOL COTTONTAIL	John Ball	80p
☐ JOHNNY GET YOUR GUN	John Ball	85p
☐ CONFESS, FLETCH	Gregory Mcdonald	90p
☐ THE TRIPOLI DOCUMENTS	Henry Kane	95p
☐ THE EXECUTION	Oliver Crawford	90p
☐ TIME BOMB	James D. Atwater	90p
☐ THE SPECIALIST	Jasper Smith	85p
☐ KILLFACTOR FIVE	Peter Maxwell	85p
☐ ROUGH DEAL	Walter Winward	85p
☐ THE SONORA MUTATION	Albert J. Elias	85p
☐ THE RANSOM COMMANDO	James Grant	95p
☐ THE DESPERATE HOURS	Joseph Hayes	90p
☐ THE MOLE	Dan Sherman	95p